THE DEVELOP

D0356684

Recent decades have witnessed unprecedented advances in research on human development. In those same decades there have been profound changes in public policy toward children. Each book in the Developing Child series reflects the importance of such research in its own right and as it bears on the formulation of policy. It is the purpose of the series to make the findings of this research available to those who are responsible for raising a new generation and for shaping policy in its behalf. We hope that these books will provide rich and useful information for parents, educators, child-care professionals, students of developmental psychology, and all others concerned with the challenge of human growth.

Jerome Bruner
New York University

Michael Cole
University of California, San Diego

Annette Karmiloff-Smith
Medical Research Council, London

SERIES EDITORS

The Developing Child Series

Daycare

REVISED EDITION

Alison Clarke-Stewart

Harvard University Press
Cambridge, Massachusetts
1993

Library of Congress Cataloging-in-Publication Data

Clarke-Stewart, Alison, 1943–
  Daycare / Alison Clarke-Stewart.—Rev. ed.
    p. cm. — (The Developing child series)
  Includes bibliographical references and index.
  ISBN 0-674-19405-5 (alk. paper).—ISBN 0-674-19406-3 (pbk. alk. paper)
  1. Day care centers. 2. Child development. 3. Day care centers—United
States. I. Title. II. Series: Developing child.
HV851.C55 1993
362.7'12—dc20
92-19515
    CIP

Preface

When I first published this book ten years ago, I never imagined that I would be writing a revision a decade later. Daycare, then, was an issue of concern to me both as a psychologist and as a new parent. Other parents and psychologists were also asking whether preschool children should be put into daycare and, if so, what kind of care. We were all concerned over the lack of quality and unsure of what was beneficial for children. Ten years later, the problems of daycare are still with us, and the situation has become even worse. There is more childcare available and more parents are using it, but the care is not of higher quality and it is not more affordable. Psychologists are still asking whether children should be in daycare at all—today the particular concern is for young infants—and parents are still having trouble finding high-quality services. These problems will not be resolved anytime soon. There must be a concerted effort to educate all Americans—those in positions of power as well as those with young children—about the importance of good daycare. This book is dedicated to that effort.

Contents

1 / The Problem

Twenty-five years ago in the United States, the ratio of men to women who showed up at the doctor's office with ulcers was twenty to one. Today it is two to one. These statistics reflect significant changes in women's lives over the past two decades, changes that have brought more and more women into the workforce and require them to perform a delicate balancing act as they juggle the demands of home, family, and work.

Today most women with children are stretched thin, working at two full-time jobs. They spend forty hours a week in employment outside the home, another thirty-six hours at home looking after the house and children, and in between they commute.[1] The average worker now spends ten hours more a week commuting and working than a generation ago. As one mother reported, "I'm always on edge because I'm so far away from my children. If there were an emergency, it would take me over an hour to get home."[2]

These women must plan and schedule their activities rigidly. They may do less housework than they would if they were not working; they may complete their household chores in less time. But they still spend almost as much time taking care of their children as they would if they were not employed. The tasks of bathing, feeding, dressing, teaching, and transporting children do not disappear just because the mother is employed.

Although husbands may help with the housework and children, there is no equal sharing of tasks between spouses. The primary responsibility and time commitment in most families is still the mother's, and even if she has hired help to assist with these tasks—a cleaning person, housekeeper, laundry service, daycare provider—it is still her responsibility to arrange for and manage such assistance. Three quarters of the mothers employed in full-time jobs claim they don't have enough time to do everything. They cope with the situation by giving up time for themselves, spending fewer hours on hobbies, reading, gardening, socializing, and other personal pleasures; they have no free time at all.

This double duty of homemaker and jobtaker takes its toll in physical and psychological stress.[3] As a result of their constant efforts to deal with the demands of family and job, most mothers holding full-time jobs feel tired and overworked. Many feel lonely and isolated. All feel harried. There are compensations, of course. They feel good about getting out into the world and having new experiences. They get more satisfaction from outside work than nonworking women do from housework. They feel better about themselves as individuals and as competent achievers. They feel healthier, more independent, and in control of their own lives. But they also feel rushed, tied down, and under pressure, especially when they are first adjusting to their dual role.

These problems are especially acute for mothers with limited resources. Mothers with low incomes must deal with the stresses of inadequate living conditions and concerns about how the family will survive, in addition to the stresses of combining work and parenthood. Single mothers must cope with the demands of work and children alone, enduring the physical strain of doing everything by themselves, the psychological strain of isolation, loneliness, and bitterness, and the economic strain of limited family income. Even with adequate resources and a partner's help, however, working mothers experience stress as they cope with physical fatigue, with conflict between their work and their husband's, and with the challenge of balancing their maternal, wifely, and working roles.

Nor do employed mothers feel as good about themselves as parents as mothers who stay home. Although they claim to be less invested in the maternal role than nonworking mothers, working mothers worry more about the time they spend with their children and feel guilty about leaving them when they have to go to work. They feel deprived of their children's company. They feel confused and worry about the harm they might be doing their children. A national panel of experts wrote:

> Parents today are worried and uncertain about how to bring up their children . . . They fear they are neglecting their children, yet they sometimes resent the demands their children make. [They] wonder whether they're doing a good job as parents, yet are unable to define just what a good job is . . . What is new . . . is the intensity of the malaise, the sense of having no guidelines or supports for raising children, the feeling of not being in control as parents, and the widespread sense of personal guilt for what seems to be going awry.[4]

In one survey, more than a third of the parents interviewed worried about how well they were raising their children. Half of the working mothers interviewed thought children were worse off if mothers were working.[5]

All these kinds of stress—fatigue, frustration, worry, guilt, uncertainty—can lead to heightened depression and anxiety, not to mention ulcers. In one study, the stress was sufficient to drive one quarter of all the mothers of young children to doctors with symptoms of depression or anxiety.[6] Psychologists have suggested that for working mothers the *dominant* role is that of mother, and only if the demands of this role are met are women able to gain satisfaction from their other role as worker. If a woman is not satisfied with both roles, this is reflected not only in her own well-being but in her behavior with her child. Women who are not happy have been found to be less involved, affectionate, playful, stimulating, and effective with their children.[7]

Central to the mother's satisfaction is the kind of arrangement she has made for the care of her children while she is at work. If mothers cannot be assured that their children are safe in their absence, they can neither concentrate on their work nor feel they are doing right by their family. Only a small minority of working mothers are able to coordinate their schedules with their partner's, so that the father can take care of the children while the mother is at work. The rest must make some other arrangement for childcare. It is critical for each of these mothers and their children that a satisfactory daycare arrangement be made.

But finding satisfactory daycare is not easy. In a study of over 8,000 employees in 33 companies and agencies in Portland, Oregon, half of the women with children under twelve reported that they had experienced stress related to childcare in the previous month.[8]

For one thing, it is difficult to know what care arrangement to make because of the wide variety of types available. Daycare may occur in the child's home or someone else's, in a home setting or a center, with an unpaid relative or a paid care provider, with a friendly neighbor or a professional nanny; the child may be in a setting with one other child or many, in a facility run by a church, a community organization, the government, or the school district, in a program that stresses education, social skills, or play. How can a parent know what type of arrangement is best?

It is also difficult to select a daycare arrangement because of the enormous differences in the quality of care offered. It ranges from merely "custodial" care, with minimal standards of safety and no program of stimulation, to "developmental" care, with frequent and fond attention from adult caregivers, a safe and interesting physical environment, and the opportunity to play with other children in a program of enriching educational experiences. Most daycare falls somewhere in between, too often toward the low end. How can parents assess the quality of the daycare arrangement? How can they be sure that the quality of the care they find is adequate?

The third reason that arranging childcare is hard is that, although these types of care are available nationwide, not all are available to every family. Each family has to make do with what it can find in its community or neighborhood, within its budget, fitting its schedule, and open to the particular child. Parents must find a satisfactory daycare arrangement that meets their particular needs, and they do not have a full range of options from which to choose. Few parents can find "model" daycare programs for their children—or afford them. The more resources they have, the better are their chances of finding adequate care. The most affluent families can afford excellent care and are more likely to find it. The poorest families are eligible for the few slots in government-supported centers. But all the families in between—the vast majority—can neither afford nor find care of such high quality.[9] They must patch together a childcare arrangement, find an acceptable daycare facility, get their child into it, monitor it, pay for it, and worry about it, drawing on whatever resources they have. In general, finding daycare is catch as catch can. Daycare is as necessary for most families as a car and a refrigerator, but infinitely harder to find and more expensive to buy.

For most families, the expense of paying for daycare is a major reason that arranging childcare is difficult. Parents spend more for childcare than for anything else except, perhaps, food, housing, and taxes. They must pay the bulk of childcare fees from their incomes, assisted only by the tax credit that allows a family to deduct between 20 and 30 percent of childcare expenses from their federal income tax, up to a maximum of $2,400 a year for one child and $4,800 a year for more children. Parents with relatively high incomes spend twice as much for childcare as poor parents, but this amounts to only about 5 percent of their income. For poor families, childcare takes a relatively bigger bite out of the monthly paycheck. Low-income families (earning under $15,000 a year) pay about one quarter of their income for childcare—as much as they pay for housing.[10]

Another reason that arranging for daycare is difficult is that "expert opinion" on the subject is divided. Child-development authorities offer parents little guidance in making decisions. Some pediatricians, politicians, child psychologists, teachers, and clergymen are enthusiastic about the possibilities that daycare offers mothers and children; others, equally eminent, are adamantly opposed to any nonparental childrearing. Some personal advisers (say, feminist friends) are likely to endorse daycare; others, just as insistent (say, mothers-in-law), are critical of it and of the mother's desire to work. This lack of consensus provides no constructive help to mothers in search of childcare.

Finally, the notion of daycare itself goes against the

traditional views of family and childrearing that our society has espoused for generations, family-oriented views that dominated the upbringing of most of today's working mothers. The working mother cannot fall back on traditional values or on her own childhood experiences for guidance. She must make decisions about daycare on her own, without expert or societal guidance, without full knowledge of what types of daycare are available and will prove most satisfactory, choosing from a limited set of options, each of unknown quality.

This book is intended to help working and would-be working mothers solve some of the problems of arranging for satisfactory daycare. It does not solve the problems, for there are no simple or universal solutions. Solutions depend on individual children, individual settings, and individual circumstances. But it does offer information that, I hope, will guide parents in solving the problems on their own.

It does this in several ways. One way is by describing the range of different kinds of daycare currently in use. A second way is by reporting the results of research on the effects of these kinds of care on children's intellectual, social, and emotional development. A third way is by giving some information about what aspects of the daycare arrangement seem to promote—or hinder—a child's development, such as the number of children in the daycare setting and their ages, the kind of equipment, the content of the program or curriculum, and the quality and training of the caregivers. The fourth way is by giving some hints about what kinds of daycare might be most suitable for individual children. And the final way is by offering some guidelines for finding and recognizing daycare settings of high quality.

But the problems of daycare go beyond individual parents and children. Providing facilities to support working mothers and their children is at least in part a responsibility of the society as a whole. For this reason the book also includes a brief discussion of the problem of daycare at the national level in the context of political, economic, and ideological forces. It documents by a brief history how daycare availability and use have always been linked to broad social issues. Finally, to expand thinking about daycare even further to include consideration of new options and to illustrate that there is no one simple solution to the problem at the national level either, it describes a few of the ways that other nations are solving their daycare problems. All of these kinds of information should help you to understand the larger issues surrounding daycare and, perhaps, encourage you to support constructive social change that would reduce daycare problems for future generations.

2 / New Needs

A number of social changes have affected the modern family and created a new need for childcare beyond what the family can provide, a need more pressing than has ever existed before. The supply of high-quality daycare services has not expanded fast enough to fill this need. It is important to find out both why the need for daycare has increased and why the supply of good care has not kept pace.

Why Daycare Is Needed

Women working. The major social change affecting the need for childcare has been the dramatic increase in the number of women who are employed in jobs outside the home. Maternal employment is fast becoming the usual pattern, and the first question upon meeting a woman at a dinner party now is usually not "How do you do?" but "What do you do?" This trend has been almost a revolutionary tide over the past twenty years. In 1970, only 30 percent of the mothers of children under six in the United States were in the workforce; today about 60 percent are, and even among mothers of children under three, about half are off at work. Now, for the first time in history, a majority of young children have working mothers. This trend is pronounced, worldwide, and expected to continue. It is estimated that, by the year 2000, 70 percent of the mothers of children under six in this country will be in the labor force. Not only is an increase in the proportion of mothers who work projected, but an increase is expected in the absolute number of working mothers. Because of a large cohort of child-bearing women, it is projected that by 1995 in the United States there will be nearly 15 million preschool children with mothers in the workforce.

What has caused this dramatic rise in maternal employment? The primary and most obvious cause is economic. The desire to maintain or improve the family's standard of living, coupled with rising costs and high inflation, has led to a need for increased income in most families. Because of the decline in real family income since 1970, two-parent families in the United States now find it necessary for both parents to work to support the family at a level that used to be achieved by one wage earner alone. Divorced, single, and widowed mothers must work to support themselves and their dependents, because child and spousal support is limited and declining. Even among those mothers who currently are at home, as many as one third would prefer to work and bring in extra income if acceptable childcare were available. In all surveys, the most common reason mothers give for working is, quite simply, that they need the money. Nevertheless, although financial needs may be foremost, there are other reasons. In one survey by the U.S. Department of Labor, 69 percent of the employed wives interviewed said they worked for the money, but 55 percent said they would continue to work even if they didn't need the money.[1] In another survey, fewer than one fifth of the working mothers interviewed said they would stop working even if there were no financial need to work.[2]

Employed mothers also work because they like their jobs, because they want to have careers, because they want to get out of the house and meet people, have new experiences, alleviate boredom or frustration, and because the feminist movement made it easier for them to work and created the expectation that they would. The women's movement contributed to the increase of working mothers by bringing pressure against job discrimination, by encouraging new employment and educational opportunities for women, and by making it fashionable for women to work. Women's liberation replaced the traditional notion of "motherhood is fulfillment" with a feminist mystique that highlighted one question: "Am I fulfilling my potential for achievement in the real world?" Feminism encouraged women to be meaningfully and gainfully employed and made many feel guilty if they "only" stayed at home doing housework and raising children. Many of these women's partners, also influenced by the feminist viewpoint and unwilling to be accused of male chauvinism, urged their wives to work. In the 1980s, the Department of Labor's *Dictionary of Occupational Titles,* which ranks 22,000 occupations according to the complexity of skills each requires, illustrated the general devaluation of housework and childcare in American society: it placed the occupation of homemaker at the lowest level, along with restroom attendant, parking-lot attendant, and poultry-offal shoveler. If this was society's attitude, no wonder more and more women felt the need to avoid the stigma of being a mere housewife.

Mothers alone. A second social trend that affected the daily care of children was the increase in the number of single-parent families. This was the result of both a rising rate of childbearing among unmarried women and a rising rate of divorce. Since the turn of the century in the United States, the number of marriages ending in divorce has increased 700 percent. Marriages now are like automobiles—short-lived and replaceable, with divorce an easy solution to an unsatisfactory relationship. Today about one half of all marriages end in divorce. Every year there are a million divorces, affecting over a million children. It is estimated that more than one half of all children born today will spend some time in a one-parent family. Like the increase in maternal employment, this trend is most striking for families with young children: the divorce rate for parents of preschool children has risen from less than 10 percent in 1950 to over 20 percent in 1990. The rise in the number of single-parent families has increased the need for daycare because, whether divorced or never married, single mothers are more likely than those in two-parent households to be employed. One survey found that 56 percent of the single mothers of preschoolers worked (more than 80 percent of them full time) as against 33 percent of married mothers.[3] Furthermore, although the remarriage rate has kept pace with the divorce rate, between marriages a divorced mother usually lives alone with her children and works full time. Then, when she remarries, she is likely to continue to work.

Fathers of limited help. But what happens when fathers are around? In many families, especially more affluent ones, fathers are able to spend more time around the house than they could a generation ago. Thus they are more available to care for the children while the mother works. They can spend more time in the home because they work shorter hours and do less physically demanding work. Women's groups and the popular media have also urged active participation by fathers in childcare. In families where the mother has a full-time job and both parents believe in equality for men and women, fathers are more involved in day-to-day childcare than they were twenty years ago.[4]

One might expect that this increase in fathers' participation in childcare would compensate for the decreased availability of care by working mothers. This is not the case. In almost all families, childcare is still considered the mother's responsibility. At best, in most families the man contributes a couple of hours a day to the running of the household. As several surveys show, while married men readily endorse the idea of equal housework, they are slow to carry out anything more than the garbage. Although 60 percent of the 700 husbands surveyed in one study voiced support for shared household responsibility, only 27 percent of them vacuumed and 29 percent helped with the laundry.[5] In another survey, parents were asked to rate 89 childrearing activities in terms of whether they should be the mother's or the father's responsibility.[6] Half of the activities were considered by the parents to be the mother's exclusive responsibility. These included all physical caretaking, behavioral training, and aesthetic enrichment. One third, having to do with education and discipline, could be shared. Only eight activities—involving guidance in traditionally masculine areas such as physical assertiveness, mechanical skills, and sports—were considered the father's responsibility.

This survey no doubt reflects both current beliefs about appropriate roles for men and women and the realities of fathers' available time. Working fathers, like working mothers, have limited time available for childcare and household tasks. The clearest predictor of the amount of time a father is likely to contribute to childcare is his work schedule, not his wife's work schedule, his income, or his belief in equality of the sexes. If the father works more than forty hours a week, he spends an average of about two hours a day on household tasks; but if he works over fifty hours a week, he typically spends only one hour on housework and childcare.[7] Fathers too are victims of the economic pressures of inflation and of increasingly higher expectations about acceptable standards of living, and although there has been some effort to promote a twenty-five-hour work week for women, there has been no such effort for fathers.

Even when employers offer parents "flexitime," so that they can tailor their work schedules to their family schedules, the roles of mothers and fathers do not change; childcare is still the mother's responsibility, and fathers still list work as their top priority.[8] As one father said, "Work makes clear objective calls on you, and the penalties if you don't meet them are explicit and obvious. The demands, requests, and pleas from your family are not. That tends to tilt the balance toward work."

Despite wishful thinking about fathers' contributions, then, in most families there is still a need for childcare beyond what the two parents together can provide.

Grandmothers gone. Another social change that has increased the need for daycare is the decreasing availability of other relatives, such as grandparents, aunts, and older siblings, who used to provide childcare. The trend observed in all western societies toward smaller and smaller families has clearly increased parents' need to find childcare outside the family. Because most families now have only two children, who are relatively close to each other in age, there are no longer older siblings available to provide care for younger brothers and sisters. Nor are there likely to be aunts or cousins who could provide childcare, because families have smaller networks of relatives.

Compounding this trend toward smaller families is increased geographic mobility. It is common now for young adults to move far away from home to marry and raise their children. This has decreased the likelihood that, even if they were available, relatives would be living near enough to provide childcare. A parallel change over the past decades has been the steady decline in the number of families who "take in" older relatives to live in the household. The possibility that grandparents or great aunts will live in the same house as parents with young children is exceedingly rare. In the average household today there are only two adults; fewer than 4 percent of American children live in three-generational families. But even if they live nearby, grandmothers and aunts increasingly have lives, homes, and jobs of their own and are less likely to be available for childcare.

Values changing. The need for new kinds of childcare has also been fostered by changes in social values regarding the appropriate roles for parents and children. There has been a marked move away from the traditional notion that parents should devote their lives to their children, making sacrifices in their own personal lives to ensure that their children will have it better than they did. In a survey of parents in 1,230 families with children under thirteen, all parents were less self-sacrificing than in the previous generation.[9] Forty-three percent of those interviewed reflected the attitudes of a "new breed" of parents, who reject conventional notions of marriage, religion, thrift, and toil. They were less child-oriented and more self-centered than their parents were and were raising their children to eat, play, dress, and do as they pleased. The goal for both parents and children in these families, it seems, is personal fulfillment. This new attitude of the "me generation" frees parents from feeling that childrearing is their exclusive duty and leads them to want and expect supplementary care for their children.

The Daycare Supply

It is clear from this catalogue of social changes that many families are finding it desirable or necessary to make arrangements for the daily care of their children beyond what they themselves can provide. More and more families are looking for more and more daycare. Is it available?

Since 1970, there has been an 80 percent increase in the number of preschool children in daycare. Every year the number of young children in some form of daycare or early education program has increased markedly, and so has the number of daycare places available. The supply of daycare center places has tripled in the past fifteen years.[10] There are now 9 million preschool children whose mothers are working and 6 million places for these children in licensed daycare centers and daycare homes. The problem is not that there is an *overall* shortage of daycare so much as that there are particular kinds of shortages. There are shortages in some geographical areas—shortages of centers in the west and in rural areas, of licensed daycare homes in the northeast and south. There is a shortage of care for infants. There are shortages of care that is affordable and of high quality. And there are shortages of one type of care that parents prefer: center care. Only a minority of those parents who want center care find openings for their children. Some mothers wait in line all through the night before registration day for the few places at a highly regarded daycare center that are filled within hours. Others rush to put their names on a waiting list at a center on the day they find out they are pregnant. Most parents who are not able to enroll their children in centers make other arrangements—with aunts, neighbors, babysitters, daycare home providers, nursery schools, or some combination of these. But there are still many thousands of children who are unsupervised or in the care of siblings under sixteen or relatives over sixty-five. Many more mothers would work or would return to work earlier if they could find adequate care for their children. The most common reason for not working is that satisfactory daycare is not available.[11]

The evidence seems clear. Social forces have created a serious need for alternatives to the traditional childcare provided by a mother at home. The need continues to increase as more and more mothers go to work without being able to rely on traditional family supports, such as babysitting big sisters and home-bound grandmothers. Although there has been an increase in daycare services over the past two decades, the supply of *good* daycare has simply not kept up with the demand.

Why Better Daycare Is Needed

The editor of a recent issue of the *Journal of Social Issues* called childcare in the United States a "national scandal" and "a most serious problem for children in our society."[12] Just how bad is the daycare available today? In the 1989 National Child Care Staffing Study, a study of 643 classrooms from 227 daycare centers in five American cities, the quality of care in the majority of centers was rated as barely adequate. Only 12 percent of the classes sampled received a rating of "good."[13] Comparable findings were obtained in the most recent comprehensive survey of childcare, *A Profile of Child Care Settings*, a telephone survey of a nationally representative sample of 583 licensed home-based childcare providers and over 2,000 center directors.[14]

A major problem identified in both these studies was staff turnover. Caregivers simply do not stay in the childcare setting very long. The rate of staff turnover in daycare settings has tripled over the past ten years. It is now common for centers to experience as much as a 50 percent turnover in staff every year. For daycare home providers, turnover is 60 percent; every year, over half of the women providing home care go out of business. This means that there is less than a fifty-fifty chance that the child's caregiver at the beginning of the year will be there at the end of the year. Such rapid rates of turnover are one indication that the quality of available daycare is not good.

Another indication of poor quality is that caregivers must look after too many children at a time. Class sizes and the ratios of children to caregivers in daycare have also increased since the late 1970s. Today the average child-adult ratio for three- and four-year-old children in daycare centers has reached the highest level recommended by early childhood professionals: ten children for every adult. This is still acceptable—but just barely. The majority of center directors and home care providers in the national Child Care Settings study reported ratios that met professional recommendations and state regulations, but a wide range of conditions was uncovered. In some centers in the survey, as many as twenty preschool children were being cared for by a single caregiver. In a number of states, the required adult-child ratio is only one adult for fifteen children.

What is more worrying, for children under three, even the *average* ratios were higher than what professionals consider acceptable. For one-year-olds, for example, the recommended ratio is one adult for every four children, but in the average classroom, caregivers were taking care of more than four children each, and it was not uncommon to find one adult taking care of five or six or even as many as eight infants. In several states it is permissible to have as many as eight infants in a daycare home. This cannot be good care. No adult, no matter how loving and attentive, can possibly provide good care for so many babies—let alone remove them safely in case of a fire. Only three states (Maryland, Massachusetts, and Kansas) require that daycare facilities have a ratio of one adult for every three infants, the ratio recommended by experts in the field. Twenty states allow ratios exceeding one adult for four infants, and in some states, the sky's the limit. In Idaho, for instance, the state-required minimum is one adult for twelve infants.

The third index of the quality of daycare is the training that caregivers have. As we shall see, caregivers who have received some training in childcare or child development are more likely to provide good care. Currently, only 27 states require that center caregivers have any training before they begin work, and less than half that number require that daycare home providers be trained. Nevertheless, the statistics on caregivers' training and education indicate improvement. In the Child Care Staffing study, 65 percent of the teachers and 56 percent of the assistant teachers had completed course work in early childhood or child development at a high school, vocational school, college, or graduate school. In the Child Care Settings study, about half of the teachers had graduated from college, and nearly all had received some child-related training. These levels of education are higher than those observed fifteen years ago. In 1976, less than one third of the teachers in full-time centers had graduated from college, and less than half had attended college at all.

But these statistics refer only to daycare center staffs. Home-based caregivers, who provide most of the daycare services today, are much less likely to have high levels of education or training in child development. Only 12 percent of the licensed home providers in the Child Care Settings study had graduated from college. We have no systematic national data on the levels of training and education of unlicensed home care providers, but suspect that they are on the average even less well trained than those who are professional enough to have obtained a license.

Obstacles to Better Daycare

Why is daycare in such a sorry state? Why haven't government or private groups stepped in to support the expansion and improvement of daycare services? Why hasn't this been a higher priority in public policy? There are many reasons, involving deep-seated psychological issues and values, economic interests, and political agendas. Daycare is no simple issue. There is not even agreement among all American citizens that daycare *should be* expanded or improved. Daycare engenders controversies that go far beyond what is convenient for mothers and strike at the core of our social system and our personal ideologies. The state of daycare reflects a national ambivalence about childcare. We have the knowledge to provide good childcare, but lack the will to do so.

Expert opinions. The experts—in child development, early childhood education, childcare—are the ones we might expect to be leading the charge for better care. They are not, because they do not themselves agree about daycare.

On one side, there are experts who paint the gloomiest possible picture of unstable babysitters, regimented daycare homes, daycare centers with twenty children for every adult and a sorry collection of broken toys. They strongly advise all mothers to stay home to provide their children with proper care and a stable human relationship. They emphasize children's need for devoted, responsive, full-time parental love and suggest that women who want to work should find careers they can follow at home. They suggest that children without a mother's full-time attention risk emotional problems. At most they recommend part-time work for mothers.

On the other side, knowledgeable professionals point to the potential benefits of daycare for mothers and children. They stress the good that daycare can do, by allowing families a higher standard of living and by giving children enriching experiences with peers and teachers. To add to the mix, some experts reverse their stand from one year to the next.

Clearly there is no consensus among the professionals, and so their opinions, published in books and magazines and expressed on radio and television shows, have increased the confusion and concern about daycare. Why do these authorities, even those who are supposedly basing their opinions on scientific evidence, disagree? The answer lies in the unavoidable tendency of everyone, professionals included, to interpret what they know in line with their own personal values.

Personal values. The values that color our views about childcare can be divided into two major camps: the "righteous right" and the "liberated left." Righteous rightists give top priority to family and home. They admire the traditional view of motherhood: mother's place is in the home, where her day can be spent guiding her children with serene and sensitive wisdom through the pitfalls of bad companions, junk food, and TV violence, to achieve the American dream of success and fulfillment, and where she can be available to greet her tired husband at day's end with a smile, soothing candlelight, and gourmet cuisine, after the charming children have been presented and put to bed. They subscribe to an ideal of self-sufficient families creating independent and unique individuals who make it on their own in a competitive society. Righteous rightists oppose daycare because it removes mother from the house and sullies her virtue in the marketplace. It removes children from home and mother. It impedes the development of children's individualism by group rearing. It encourages families to rely on others for assistance in childcare rather than maintaining their own vital self-sufficiency. It intrudes into families' privacy.

Liberated leftists place at the top of their priorities the rights of women and the poor. They maintain that citizens and governments have a responsibility to uphold these rights for all. The myth of motherhood they have created is the feminist ideal of mother as interesting, happy, and satisfied because she can attain fulfillment in a dynamic career or meaningful work. They support daycare because they see it as a way of liberating women from the bonds of childrearing and offering them equal rights. Daycare increases the self-sufficiency of families by enabling them to earn larger incomes, and it promotes individual achievement by providing educational services for children who otherwise would not have such intellectual stimulation.

Liberated left and righteous right are, of course, stereotypes of the two extremes in personal values. Most people fall in between or waffle back and forth. Nevertheless, with the diversity these values reflect, it is not surprising that society has failed to reach agreement about supporting, expanding, or improving daycare.

Economics. There are also more tangible obstacles to providing daycare. The major one is economic. Although the need for daycare services is enormous, so are the costs. Parents are already paying a lot for daycare, but the real cost of high quality childcare is several times greater than what parents currently pay. It has been calculated, for example, that the real cost of providing infant care, if providers were paid an appropriate wage, would be over $1,000 a month for each infant. Undoubtedly there are some parents who can afford to pay $1,000 a month, but most cannot. Low salaries force many providers who are well trained and love their work out of the field. Low wages were the most common reason given in the Child Care Staffing study for caregivers leaving their positions. Childcare workers are abysmally underpaid relative to their levels of education. They earn less than half what comparably educated women in other professions earn, less than one third as much as comparably educated men. Sixty percent earn less than $5 an hour; the average annual wage of a daycare center teacher is just over the poverty threshold for a family of three ($9,000); and 90 percent of daycare home providers earn less than poverty-level wages.[15] Childcare workers have never been well paid, but their wages have decreased over 20 percent in the last decade. They are now the second most underpaid workers in the United States, next to the clergy, according to the National Committee on Pay Equity. And of course they have no health insurance or retirement plan. As caregivers leave childcare for better-paying positions, the quality of daycare diminishes.

Daycare is an expensive service, and it is hard to

reduce costs without reducing quality. Economists have concluded that daycare, like education and health care, cannot be adequately provided on a fee-for-service basis. It requires some subsidy from government, charity, or industry. But it is difficult to get financial support for any social service when the economy is plagued by inflation, recession, and a deficit budget, and few service-oriented organizations—unions, churches, charitable agencies—are willing to invest in daycare. At the present time, the federal government spends about $8 billion a year on childcare. It sounds enormous, but half of this money is in the form of a tax credit for parents and does not pay directly for care or for improving care. Another quarter is the money that goes to pay for Head Start, which is not a full-day program and so does not meet working mothers' need for daycare. Some $1 billion goes to the childcare food program for low-income families. Less than $1 billion is given to the states for their social services. The states use the funds primarily to purchase low-cost childcare and to support training and counseling services for low-income mothers. High costs and insufficient funding are thus major impediments to providing adequate childcare.

Politics. Another obstacle is political: daycare is not represented by a powerful interest group. There are many splits, not only between daycare supporters and opposers but even among the supporters of daycare—splits over who should staff daycare facilities, who should regulate daycare, who should administer funds for daycare, who should have priority for using daycare, and so on. There is a clear need for more trained personnel in daycare, but who should they be? There are divisions among those who would promote staffing daycare with schoolteachers, early childhood educators, social workers, nurses, or hold-ers of two-year degrees from community colleges. With the decline in the number of schoolage children and the desire to bolster their own positions, teachers and their unions point to the benefits of existing administrative systems and available trained personnel in the public school system. Just as adamantly, opponents of this perceived takeover by the educational establishment point to the disadvantages of a system mired in bureaucracy and overpaid teachers who are trained to work with older children.

There also are splits about who should regulate daycare—the federal government, state governments, local city, municipal, or county governments, or simply parents themselves—and there are disagreements about what the regulations should contain. In the 1970s, there was a long, drawn-out battle over daycare standards, which involved hundreds of daycare providers, parents, child-development experts, and legislators, and dozens of hearings, laws, and revisions. The participants argued about costs, quality, space, size, nutrition, health care, staff training, adult-child ratios, monitoring, and reporting. Eventually they agreed on some guidelines for minimal daycare standards (described in Chapter 9), but these guidelines were never implemented. In the last several years, a coalition of some eighty groups concerned about childcare, including the American Psychological Association, the American Academy of Pediatrics, and the American Federation of Teachers, has lobbied for more support and legislation for childcare. Their efforts so far have met with little success, limited again by political and economic issues.

Fears about children's well-being. Yet another obstacle to providing daycare services is the fear that daycare harms children. This is based not just on personal values but on early studies of children in residential institutions, such as orphanages and asylums. These studies painted a grim picture. Institutionalized children died at a staggering rate: in Dublin in the eighteenth century, for example, of 10,000 children admitted to a foundling home, only 45 survived. In the nineteenth century, with advances in hygiene and medical care, the mortality rate for children in institutions was greatly improved, but even in the early part of our century physicians were still noting that the children were scrawny, apathetic, and severely retarded. At the time, these problems were attributed to "bad blood," and nothing was done to change the situation. Only in the 1940s was it recognized that something about the environment in these institutions might be responsible for the dire outcomes observed. The something fixed on was the lack of a mother's love. It is this old view that has sometimes been used in arguments against daycare, by suggesting that children of working mothers who are in full-time daycare will be similarly deprived of maternal love.

But children in daycare are not deprived of maternal love or even maternal care; they have that love and care before they are placed in daycare and continue to experience it at the end of every day. Mothers don't put their children in daycare because they don't love them. What is more, the retarded children in institutions were deprived of much more than maternal love: they had little affection or attention from anyone. Attendants were few and always changing; they could not give individual children continuous, consistent, warm, or responsive care. The physical surroundings were poor, with minimal health care, inadequate food, and nothing interesting to look at or play with. There were no programs of education or exercise. These extreme conditions are not found in daycare centers today. Studies of residential institutions, whether old or new, simply cannot be used to suggest that daycare is harmful to children's development.

Still, fears persist about the harmful effects of daycare. One concern focuses on the relationship between child and mother. Psychologists have demonstrated that it is essential to healthy emotional development for an infant to have a close and continuing relationship with one caring adult over the first several years of life. The question is, does that adult have to be the mother? Or if it is the mother, does she have to be the child's exclusive caregiver? How many adult caregivers can be involved before it becomes too much for the child? What will it mean if children are raised by strangers or professionals rather than by family? After a close relationship with the mother or professional is established, is it harmful for the child to be separated from that adult? What will happen if children are cared for by a changing cast of caregivers who have different childrearing styles and values? In the absence of solid answers to these questions, many parents and professionals fear the worst.

They also wonder what effect daycare will have on children's intellectual development. Researchers have demonstrated that stimulation in the form of adult attention, conversation, and play is critical for children's intellectual development in the preschool years. Can sufficient adult attention be given each child to ensure intellectual growth in a daycare facility with a large group of children and few caregivers? And what about the child's social development? We have all observed that even very young children behave quite differently when they are with other children than when they are with their parents. Will children who are raised in groups be more dependent on their peers? Will they be more aggressive toward other children? Will they be withdrawn and passive? Will they conform to normal adult standards for socially acceptable behavior, such as courtesy and cooperation? Will they learn to control their impulses? Will they retain their individuality? Once again, many fear the worst.

Sheer ignorance. One last obstacle to improving daycare is people's ignorance about its importance. Daycare has a bad reputation in the United States. It has filled multiple roles throughout American history, but basically it has always been something for poor, inadequate families. In the beginning, daycare was for children of immigrant, single mothers. Later it was part of the War on Poverty, a vehicle for the uplifting of disadvantaged children or their parents. Most recently it has become a means of allowing welfare mothers to get jobs. Daycare has never been viewed as a right of children or a need of working parents. Nor has it been viewed as a potentially educational institution for all young children. It has not been considered an important component of the ecology of childhood or a critical contributor to children's well-being. Many have failed to appreciate that children's experiences in daycare may have lasting effects on their development. They do not realize how important high-quality care is. They do not understand the importance of adult-child ratios or the need for caregivers to receive training in childcare. As one New York legislator said to a lobbying group, "My grandmother raised six children, and she didn't have a college degree." Ignorance of daycare is another obstacle that must be overcome before care in this country can be strengthened.

In sum, all these problems and controversies—divergent personal values, varied expert opinions, practical and political obstacles and conflicts, fears and ignorance about the effects of daycare on children's development—have held back daycare provision. The problems are profound, unlikely to be resolved easily. Two basic kinds of change are needed before daycare can expand in any meaningful way. One would involve the dissemination of research results showing how daycare affects children. The other would be broader social and economic changes that would overcome the practical obstacles to daycare provision. In the past, there have been some booms in daycare, and major, if temporary, expansion has occurred. Perhaps it will again. In the next chapter we look back over the past century and a half to see how daycare services have waxed and waned along with other social changes.

3 / History

Daycare and its problems are not new. The history of daycare as a formal, recognized service goes back well into the last century. Since the founding of the first daycare center in the United States in 1838, the popularity of nonparental childcare has increased and decreased with changes in social, economic, and political circumstances. It is useful to consider the history of daycare in order to understand how the current situation has evolved and what the future is likely to hold.[1]

The first day nursery. The first day nurseries were a response to the flood of immigration that brought more than five million foreign families to the United States between 1815 and 1860, and to the industrialization and urbanization that took women from their homes to factories during this period. Young children were left to fend for themselves—locked up at home, allowed to roam the streets, or put under the casual supervision of a neighbor or relative. The situation was ripe for philanthropic intervention, and wealthy women and well-meaning service organizations, appalled by the neglect, vice, and lack of sanitation, organized day nurseries to provide care for these children. The first American day nursery was opened in Boston in 1838 by Mrs. Joseph Hale to provide care for the children of seamen's working wives and widows. Sixteen years later, the Nurses and Children's Hospital in New York City opened its version of the day nursery to care for infants and toddlers of working women who had been patients there. Then a day nursery was opened in Philadelphia in 1863 to care for children of working women in hospitals and factories during the Civil War. Finally, in 1893 a model day nursery set up at the World's Fair in Chicago cared for 10,000 children of visitors. By 1898, about 175 day nurseries were operating in various parts of the country, enough to warrant the creation of a National Federation of Day Nurseries.

Over the next decade, expansion of daycare continued. Day nurseries were most often set up in converted homes. They were open six days a week, twelve hours a day. Most of them were simply custodial, run by overworked matrons with one or two assistants, who had to do the laundry, cooking, and cleaning as well as looking after the children. Day nurseries did not have the benefit of public support, monetary or ideological; the day nursery was considered a last resort for children who couldn't be cared for at home.

A few day nurseries with more energetic directors offered not only clean, safe places to keep children but something of interest to occupy their time. Since the clients were largely immigrants, these centers taught children manners and hygiene in the American mode. Children were trained to use a napkin, to eat in silence, to march in line, and were given tickets to exchange for articles of clothing if they exhibited the virtues of punctuality, obedience, industry, cleanliness, and good behavior. Beginning in the 1890s, some day nurseries also began to offer a modest educational program, by hiring kindergarten teachers to come in and teach the children for several hours a day. The "curriculum" was extended in these exceptional day nurseries to include weaving, sewing, reading, spelling, and basketmaking.

Underlying the establishing of these nurseries was the notion that mothers needed help, and clients were selected on that basis. Consequently, working mothers were also offered services beyond a place to leave their children. They were offered classes in sewing, cooking, English, and childcare, access to job training and opportunities, and help with practical family problems. In the 1920s they were also given help with family-centered psychological problems.

The 1930s and 1940s. In 1933, to alleviate effects of the great depression, President Roosevelt initiated the Federal Economic Recovery Act and the Work Projects Administration. Public funds for the expansion of daycare became available for the first time. The reason was to supply jobs for unemployed teachers, nurses, cooks, and janitors. By 1937 these programs had set up 1,900 day nurseries, caring for 40,000 children. The nurseries were most commonly located in schools and followed school hours; there was increased participation by teachers and an increased emphasis on the older—educable—preschool child.

This daycare "boomlet" was short-lived, however. With the demise of the WPA in 1938, day nurseries declined until World War II. Then, with the massive mobilization of women into war-related industries and renewed financial support provided by the Lanham Act (1942), the prejudice against working women (superseded, apparently, by patriotism) disappeared, and day nurseries flourished once more. By 1945, more than a million and a half children were in daycare. This time, the programs were more innovative. In Los Angeles, for example, the Gale Manor Apartments turned its ground floor into a combination nursery and playground and accepted as tenants only working parents with children. In Portland, Oregon, the Kaiser Shipbuilding Corporation opened two daycare centers, one at the entrance to each of its shipyards, and these centers not only provided supervision for the children of women working in the shipyards but their staffs did shopping and mending, made doctors' appointments for the mothers, cared for children during minor illnesses, and offered carryout dinners at low cost to mothers who worked long hours.

From 1950 to 1965. This daycare boom ended as precipitously as it had begun, with the end of the war and the withdrawal of Lanham funds in 1946. Nearly 3,000 centers closed, and by 1950 only 18,000 children were in daycare centers. From 1950 to 1965, daycare again became a marginal service for the poor with an emphasis on social work and problem families. Unexpectedly, although the centers closed, women did not return as anticipated to their "rightful" place in the home. They continued to work, and those who were not poor enough to qualify for publicly supported daycare used the few available private centers or made other arrangements with relatives, neighbors, or housekeepers. Only in the mid-1960s did attitudes toward daycare begin to become more positive as it was recognized that mothers were already working and it seemed that provision of daycare would allow more women to get off the welfare rolls. Federal support for daycare became available once more, though still only for poor families. This change in attitude and legislation was influenced also by what was happening in early childhood education, for in the mid-1960s the two streams of services to children, day nurseries and nursery schools, began to converge.

Nursery schools. While day nurseries were supposed primarily to solve the problems of the poor, nursery schools were intended to provide enrichment for the affluent. The first cooperative nursery school was started by faculty wives at the University of Chicago in 1915. Its purpose was to offer their youngsters an opportunity for wholesome play, to give the mothers some hours of leisure away from the children, and to try a social venture of cooperation. The idea caught on quickly, and many more schools started up in the following two decades. Most of these early nursery schools were all-day programs (8:30 to 4:30), located in converted residences, and supported by parent fees and participation. Children as young as eighteen months were fed, toileted, amused, and given social training. Parent education was often part of the program and parent participation was required, but nursery schools were above all for children. They offered a rich physical environment with blocks, sand, clay, and paints where children could play freely on their own without their mothers' supervision, under the kindly guidance of an educated but unintrusive teacher, whose purpose was to help the children develop impulse control, verbal skills, and knowledge about the world. Nursery schools were popular with middle-class families from the 1930s to the 1960s.

Convergence in the late 1960s. In the late 1960s a new focus on the preschool period added energy to nursery-school education. As an outgrowth of the furor surrounding the launching of Sputnik and Americans' desire to catch up, people focused their attention on early childhood as a critical period for stimulating intellectual development. They hoped for later benefits in scientific progress and national achievement. From 1967 to 1970, enrollment in nursery schools and voluntary kindergartens increased markedly (from one quarter to one half of all eligible three- to five-year-olds), and enrollment in licensed daycare centers doubled. At the same time, these programs shifted to a more developmental, academic emphasis, and a number of experimental programs designed specifically to foster children's intellectual growth were set up. Most significantly, in 1965 a new national program that provided nursery-school education for poor children was instituted—Head Start. This project was the first major governmental involvement in early childhood programs, except in times of national emergency. It was only a part-day program and did not really serve the needs of working mothers, but it was significant because it focused public attention on the idea that education was important for all young children, not just those in affluent families. It also opened the possibility of government support for educational daycare. At the same time, in this climate of anticipation of the benefits of early childhood education, child-development professionals, middle-class parents, and women's groups were pressing for educational or "developmental" daycare. Public funds for daycare were made available through a variety of federal programs.

Not only was the federal government actively involved in funding and administering these programs, it was also involved in setting standards for them. In 1968, after much debate, the Federal Interagency Day Care Requirements were published. The requirements specified acceptable levels of staff training, safety and sanitation, health and nutrition, educational and social services, parent involvement, adult-child ratios, and group sizes. Although it was not mandated that centers must comply with the requirements, not complying was grounds for suspension or termination of any federal funds that a center was receiving. Such action was never taken, however, because compliance was financially impossible for many programs and enforcement would have led to many closings.

The 1970s and 1980s. By the beginning of the 1970s, daycare was on many people's minds, and efforts to support more and better services were becoming stronger. The 1970 White House Conference on Children selected daycare as the most serious problem confronting American families. Concerned child-development experts, childcare advocates, and representatives of the Senate and House of Representatives were developing the Comprehensive Child Development Act. In 1971, this act was accepted by Congress. It called for establishing a national network of childcare facilities available to all children and adhering to a uniform set of standards. It recommended comprehensive and educational daycare not only for poor and handicapped children but for all children, on a sliding fee scale.

This comprehensive act was the high point of childcare legislation in the history of the United States. But hopes of a national childcare system were short-lived. In December 1971 President Nixon vetoed the bill because he thought it would lead to the demise of the American family: "[the legislation] would commit the vast moral authority of the National Government to the side of communal approaches of childrearing over against the family-centered approach."

After that, childcare provision in the United States started to go downhill. In 1975 the ratio requirements outlined in the Federal Interagency Day Care Requirements were suspended, and in 1981, under President Reagan's administration, direct federal funding for childcare services was cut and the federal requirements were eliminated completely. The states became completely responsible for regulating and monitoring childcare; private businesses and individuals became responsible for paying for it. Welfare mothers could deduct money for childcare from other earned income; self-supporting families could deduct a portion of what they spent for childcare from their taxable income. Employers could set aside money for childcare from their employees' taxable income and could depreciate their physical facilities if they provided childcare. The only direct federal support for childcare was food subsidies to daycare centers and homes for low-income children, block grants to states and communities for social services to low-income families, and continued funding of Head Start. But Head Start serves less than one fifth of the children who are eligible, and it does not fill parents' need for daycare.

Overall, the results of the federal government's withdrawal from daycare were negative. Although in some states funding for childcare increased and growth in school-based programs occurred, most states raised fees, cut back services, reduced their standards, made the standards apply to fewer institutions (for example, church-related or part-time centers were exempted), and enforced the standards less stringently and consistently. Discrepancies between states increased. This led to an increase in the diversity of childcare options—a goal of the Reagan administration—but reduction in federal spending cut back the options of low-income families, especially those preferring center-based care. It also led to a decline in the quality of care available to poor parents. Private daycare programs, which increased in availability as public ones decreased, operate more efficiently and economically than publicly funded programs because they have larger classes and pay teachers lower wages—and, as a consequence, they offer lower-quality care.

Through the 1980s, fifteen to twenty daycare-related bills were presented to Congress every session. Only a handful passed, and none resulted in comprehensive daycare. The official policy in the United States continued to be federal subsidies for childcare for the poor through social security, and tax credits for childcare for everyone else. Despite the lack of government initiative, daycare enrollment grew, with private enterprise taking up the burden of daycare provision.

The 1990s. But now the tide may be turning again. An unprecedented degree of federal activity has been focused on childcare in the last few years, reflecting a consensus that a major expansion of childcare support is necessary. In 1990 Congress considered over a hundred childcare bills. One of them was a new comprehensive bill—the Act for Better Childcare (ABC Bill). This act would have established an Office of Child Care in the Department of Health and Human Services, with over $10 billion poured into daycare in four years. It would have provided incentives for states to improve the quality of all types of care for all families. It would have given more tax credits for parents and daycare providers, offered services to low-income families, provided assistance to providers in getting liability insurance, and set up a committee to draft model childcare standards for states to follow or adapt. Standards for ratios and group sizes would initially be based on the current median levels across the states. The minimal standard for caregiver qualification would have been at least fifteen hours per year of in-service training, and states would have been directed to work with institutions of higher learning to develop training for daycare personnel. States would also have been directed to develop effective licensing procedures so that inspections of facilities and providers could be done in a timely manner. Licensing staff would have been directed to make at least one unannounced annual inspection of each center and to do so for at least 20 percent of the state's daycare homes.

The bill that finally passed Congress was far less ambitious than this, but it was a step in the right direction. In October 1990 legislation was passed that provides block grants to states and refundable tax credits for low-income, single, working parents. The bill was aimed at increasing the availability of childcare and increasing parents' purchasing power as consumers of childcare. It did not reflect concerns about improving daycare quality. These concerns were addressed only in a small "quality improvements" section of the block grant legislation. As a result, poor parents will have expanded choices of childcare, but their children may or may not have a better chance of being enrolled in good care.

Childcare continues to be a patchwork quilt, varying from state to state and family to family. All states regulate daycare centers, but there is no agreement on the level of regulation or the standards that are followed. In most states, regulation consists of an annual inspection to get a license to operate, and exceptions are made for church-run and part-day programs. But standards vary widely from state to state. In Massachusetts, principal teachers in each class have to be trained in child development and the staff-child ratio for infants is one caregiver for three infants. In Georgia, teachers need a high-school diploma, and the staff-child ratio for infants is one adult for seven infants. Staff-child ratios for four-year-olds range from 1:5 to 1:20 in different states. The level of support the state government puts into daycare also varies widely.

States also determine whether daycare homes will be regulated and, if so, what standards will be followed. Licensing is required or available in only about one half of the states. But even in those states that license homes, the vast majority of care providers operate "underground." Estimates suggest that about 90 percent of home daycare is unlicensed.

From its beginning, daycare has followed economic and political currents. In the next chapter, we look at the current state of daycare, the product of these historical twists and turns.

4/ Here and Now

We have seen that the need for childcare far exceeds the supply of licensed facilities offering high-quality daycare. What arrangements have parents made as a result of this shortage? What is the current state of daycare in the United States?

Forms of Daycare

Table 1 shows the distribution of the major types of care arrangements currently being used by working mothers of preschool children in the United States. About one quarter of the families in which mothers work manage to cover childcare by juggling the parents' schedules or by taking the child along to work. Another quarter use relatives—aunts, grandmothers, older siblings. Care by relatives is especially common for infants, for poor children, and for children whose mothers work part time. A few families use a nonrelated caregiver who comes to or lives in their home—neighbor, friend, paid or unpaid babysitter, nanny, housekeeper, maid, live-in student, or *au pair*. The use of nonrelated babysitters in the child's own home has dropped sharply over the past decade. Only about 6 percent of families today use this kind of care. Again, this form of daycare is relatively more com-

Table 1. Primary Childcare Arrangements Used by Employed
Mothers for Children under Five Years

Type of care	Percent using the arrangement	
	For infants and toddlers	For preschool children
Parents themselves	25%	23%
Another relative	27	21
Nonrelated in-home provider	7	5
Daycare home	26	18
Daycare center	16	33

Statistics based on the most recent available data from the U.S.
Department of Labor.

mon for infants. About one quarter of the children whose
mothers work are cared for by a nonrelated provider
who looks after a number of children, perhaps including
her own, in her home. This "family daycare" arrangement is the most common type of care for one- and
two-year-olds whose mothers work full time. The number of regulated, licensed daycare homes in the United
States has increased by one third over the past fifteen
years.

Daycare centers are used relatively rarely for infants
and toddlers; only 16 percent of the infants of working
mothers are in centers. But for three- and four-year-olds
whose mothers work full time, centers are the daycare
arrangement of choice. About one third of the three- and
four-year-olds whose mothers work are in centers. In
addition, many children whose mothers are not employed attend daycare centers or nursery schools; currently about half of all three- and four-year-olds in the
United States attend some kind of center program. It is
in the use of daycare centers that we see the greatest
change over the past two decades. Just over the last six

years, both the capacity of daycare centers and the proportion of working mothers placing their infants in them
have doubled. Over the past fifteen years, the capacity
of daycare centers has tripled.

Care in the Child's Home

Care by a care provider (most often a relative) in the
child's own home while the mother is at work may be a
common form of daycare, but it is the one about which
we know least. It simply has not been studied—perhaps
because it is so private, or it varies so much from home
to home, or it is most often a family affair, or it seems to
be much like care by the mother.

It is obvious that, compared to other more formal
kinds of daycare, in-home care offers many advantages.
The hours are flexible; there is no need for the child or
parent to travel; the child remains in a familiar, secure
place; and the mother, to some extent, is able to monitor
the behavior of a caregiver who, if not one already, becomes like one of the family. In-home care keeps siblings
together, and the caregiver can provide each child with
individual attention. This care arrangement may be relatively economical if there are several children in the
family, if care is provided as a favor to the parents or out
of a sense of family duty, or if other services like shopping or laundry are included. If the in-home caregiver is
related to the child, this turns out to be the most stable
of all daycare arrangements.[1]

On the other hand, the arrangement also has disadvantages. The caregiver is usually untrained and unlicensed and may or may not provide good care. If she is
trained, in-home care becomes the most expensive kind
of daycare. It is difficult to find in-home caregivers because a systematic referral system for sitters and nannies

does not exist, and this form of care is the least stable if the caregiver is not a relative. Frequently having to replace caregivers is a frustrating drawback to in-home care. There is also a disadvantage for the child because educational or group activities with peers are less likely. Beyond these obvious advantages and disadvantages, daycare in the child's home is an unknown commodity of infinite variety.

Family Daycare

A second kind of home daycare is family daycare—care by a care provider in her home rather than the child's. A daycare home may be licensed or unlicensed; the care provider may be related to the child or unrelated, trained or untrained. The number of children in the daycare home may range from one to six (family daycare home) or six to twelve (group daycare home). On the average, there are six children in the daycare home. The basis for this arrangement varies from an informal agreement about shared caregiving between friends to a formal, supervised network of licensed daycare homes. Most home providers work alone, but 40 percent have partners or helpers.[2] The cost of family daycare ranges from $2,000 to $6,000 per child per year for full-time care (in 1990 dollars).

Family daycare has a number of distinct advantages as a form of care. Family daycare homes are the most numerous, least expensive, and most elastic daycare arrangement. There is no need for construction of a facility, no need to set up a complex administrative structure. Daycare homes are usually located near the child's home, and so they are easy to get to and are in a familiar neighborhood where people are likely to share the parents' values and circumstances. The mother has more control over what happens to her child in a daycare home than she would in a center because she can give instructions to a home provider that she would not be able to give a center teacher. Studies show that parents using family daycare are more likely to have a close personal relationship with the care provider than are parents using center care. They talk to the care provider more and say that they would "keep in touch" with her after the child leaves the daycare home.[3] A daycare home provider is usually flexible about taking children of different ages and in adjusting her hours to the mother's schedule. She may accept children with special needs or handicaps who would not be accepted in a center. For a family with one or two children, a daycare home is also a relatively economical form of care.

For children, a daycare home offers the advantages of providing new experiences they would not have at home and fostering relations with people outside the family, while at the same time providing continuity with the kind of family care the child is used to, in a home with a "mother figure." Family daycare offers the child the opportunity to interact with a handful of other children, of different ages, rather than overwhelming the child with a large group of agemates. Often the caregivers in a daycare home include the man of the house, and this can be another advantage over care with an in-home provider or in a center. A daycare home provider, like an in-home caregiver, can devote individual attention to the children she is looking after. If the provider is licensed or participates in a training and support network, a daycare home is relatively stable and adheres to health and safety standards. If the care provider is in a network, she is likely to be given training in childcare and regular consultation with child development professionals. The network may be affiliated with a school, university, or daycare center. In the national Child Care Settings study, about half of the regulated home providers reported that they met regularly with other care providers, and one quarter were sponsored by an agency that organizes family daycare in their area.

But this kind of daycare has disadvantages as well. A major disadvantage is that a home provider is the least accountable to parents for her actions. Daycare homes are private, and not open for public inspection. After the mother drops off her children, although she may instruct the care provider about how she wants the child taken care of, she has no knowledge of what really happens. Children may be screamers, but they are not squealers. The vast majority of daycare home providers are not trained, not licensed, and not members of a support network. They are unlikely to offer the children organized educational activities, and the physical equipment they have is not as plentiful or as varied as in most daycare centers.

Most daycare homes tend to be informal, unprofessional, and short-lived. They offer experiences for the child ranging from concerned and competent care by an involved and happy care provider to neglectful or even abusive care by a depressed and isolated woman who believes she has no marketable skills but needs the money and so takes in babies. Slightly more than half of the home providers in the Child Care Settings study said they were providing childcare so they could earn money: one third said they were doing it so they could stay home with their own children; one fifth said they were doing it as a business; and one third said it was because they liked children.

One of the first studies of daycare homes was a survey of daycare homes and centers throughout the United States carried out by the National Council of Jewish

Women.[4] Their report, published in 1972, rated daycare homes from poor to superior. Fourteen percent of the daycare homes they visited were rated as poor. For example, they found "seven or eight children, one year or under, most strapped to kitchen chairs, all seemingly in a stupor." Forty-eight percent were rated fair, 31 percent good, and only 7 percent superior. A number of studies since that one have made more systematic and detailed observations in daycare homes.[5] The largest was the National Day Care Home Study, which included 350 daycare homes in twenty-five cities, with more detailed interviews and observations made in Los Angeles, San Antonio, and Philadelphia. Putting together the findings from all these studies gives us a picture of life in a typical daycare home.

Nearly all daycare home providers offer all-day care and give the children lunch and snacks. The daycare home is usually a single-family house with an outdoor play area. Most daycare homes have no more than three children present at one time. These children tend to be in the 18- to 36-month range. In nearly half of the daycare homes, the children include one of the home provider's own. The typical daycare home provider is married, in her thirties, a high-school graduate with six years of childcare experience. Her husband is stably employed and makes a comfortable income. She is providing daycare because she is fond of children as well as for the money. She provides a positive, supportive environment: in the National Day Care Home Study, 94 percent of the home providers were observed to smile and laugh with the children; only 31 percent of them scowled or acted angry while the observer was present. All providers controlled the children by giving them directions and suggestions rather than by physically punishing them—at least while the observer was looking. On the average they spent about half of their time involved with the children and the rest of the time on housework or personal activities. When they interacted with the children, in addition to feeding, washing, and dressing them, the home providers chatted, labeled objects, explained and demonstrated how things work, read stories, and played games. They did not give formal lessons. The children spent about half their time playing alone with sand, water, clay, and toys. Usually they were actively involved in this play, not crying, fighting, or aimlessly wandering about. They interacted with the caregiver only 13 percent of the time they were in the home and with peers only 5 percent of the time. Although in most daycare homes the children watched some television, overall they spent only 7 percent of their time doing so.

Of course these are just averages. There really is no typical daycare home. There is an infinite variety of daycare homes and providers, just as there is an infinite variety of in-home providers and mothers. In age, the daycare home providers in the Day Care Home Study ranged from twenty to sixty-nine; their education ranged from junior high to college graduation; they had spent time ranging from one month to thirty-six years providing childcare.

There was also great variation in the kind of care they provided, related to whether they were licensed or part of a training network and to how much they viewed themselves as professional caregivers. Daycare home providers who were licensed, or, even better, part of a network, and who considered themselves childcare professionals, who read childcare books, went to meetings, took classes in child development, and kept records on the children they were looking after, were more likely to talk, help, teach, and play with the children and to provide a physical environment with more music, dancing, books, educational TV, and nutritious food. Daycare home providers who were doing it only because no better job was available, or as an informal agreement with friends, neighbors, or relatives, were less interactive and stimulating and spent more time on housework.

Most daycare home providers see their role as providing for children's physical needs, not as offering them education, play, and enrichment or as being sensitive to their feelings and problems. When researchers in one study asked providers what sort of person makes a good home caregiver, the typical responses received were:

> "Someone with lots of patience and time. You've got to be able to cope with all sorts of children."
> "I think you must never promise them anything you can't fulfill, and be fair to them and tolerant."
> "Someone who doesn't mind having kids running around. It's no good if you want the house to look just so."[6]

These responses suggest a view of caregiving as warm-hearted, accepting, and relatively passive. Few of the providers interviewed mentioned any outgoing qualities. Less than one fifth, for example, suggested that the provider should be prepared to play with or talk to children on their own level, and only four suggested that she should be imaginative or have ideas for doing things with children. Most thought that she should know about first aid, have common sense or experience bringing up her own children, and know something about children's play. Knowing about children's feelings or problems (such as illnesses or special needs) was mentioned infrequently.

Children in the daycare home were incorporated into the provider's family, not given special attention. Only 30 percent of the care providers in this study reported that they had carried out specific educational or play activities with the children, such as painting, reading, cutting out, playing with plasticine, blocks, or tiddly-winks, on the previous day. Instead the children watched TV, played outside, and went along shopping. Life at a daycare home is more like life at home than life at school, but it offers children less interaction with an adult than they would probably have with their mother at home. The suggestion that a daycare home is a home away from home and not a school is reflected in the fact that three quarters of the home providers in the Child Care Settings study reported that their main goal was to provide a warm, loving environment for children; only 7 percent said that the goal was to foster children's development, and only 6 percent said it was to prepare children for school.

Daycare Centers

A daycare center is the most visible and easily identified childcare arrangement, the one most people are referring to when they speak of "daycare." A center may provide care for fewer than fifteen children or more than three hundred; on the average there are about sixty children in a center. About a third of children in centers attend full time (at least 35 hours a week). They are usually divided into classes or groups according to age. The average size of these groups is 7 infants, 10 toddlers, or 14 preschoolers. Group sizes vary enormously, however. In the Child Care Staffing study, group sizes ranged from 2 to 18 for infants, from 2 to 30 for toddlers, and from 3 to 37 for preschoolers. Most children in daycare centers are three or four years old. Teachers in the centers tend to be young and of the same race as the children. They are almost inevitably women (97 percent) and under 40 years old (80 percent). Most have attended college. Parents pay from $2,600 to $5,200 yearly for a three- or four-year-old child in full-time care.

Compared to other daycare arrangements, centers have certain advantages. For the most part, they are relatively stable, keep predictable hours, and are publicly accountable and easily monitored by parents. Daycare centers don't quit or get sick or go on vacation. They usually have some staff with training in child development and are likely to offer children educational opportunities and the chance to play with other children in a child-oriented, child-sized, safe environment that is rich in materials and equipment. They may offer health services as well.

On the other hand, daycare centers are often located at some distance from the child's home, have less flexible hours, do not offer care for sick children, are more expensive, and are less available because of strict eligibility criteria. Still, all other things equal, the majority of parents prefer centers for their preschool children. They like them because of their reliability, because they offer the child learning experiences, and because those experiences change as the child gets older. Parents using centers do not change to using daycare homes. The fees parents pay for care in centers and daycare homes are about the same.

Like daycare homes, centers run the gamut from poor to excellent. In the study by the National Council of Jewish Women, 30 percent of the centers visited were rated as poor. For example, "over 20 children huddled in too small, poorly ventilated, cement floor area" or "babies kept in 'cages'—double-decker cardboard cribs in one room with open gas heater." Forty-three percent were rated fair, 21 percent good, and only 5 percent superior. These ratings were even lower than the ratings of daycare homes made in the study. But it is not fair to jump to the conclusion that center care is worse than home care. A range of quality is found in both kinds of setting.

More recent and extensive studies have attempted to detail the differences in the "ecology" of these two forms of daycare.[7] They show that, on the average, physical conditions (space, ventilation, light, toilets, cleanliness, toys, safety, nutrition, and immunization) are better in daycare centers, while daycare homes rank higher in social-personal conditions (fewer children per adult, more interaction with the caregiver, more conversation, more socialization attempts, more emotional input, and more sensitive approaches to the child by the caregiver). Learning occurs in both settings, but it is likely to be of different kinds: in the daycare homes there was more free exploration, "messing around," casual learning in real-life tasks with real role models. A question from the caregiver, "What would you like for lunch?" could lead to a long discussion about finding something everyone likes, which foods are more nutritious, what ingredients are necessary, how long it takes to prepare, and so on. In centers there were more interactions among children, more formal educational activities, more questions from the caregiver, and more rules to follow. A comment about food might lead to a "mini lesson" consisting of questions posed by the teacher: "Are peas a vegetable?" "How many vegetables can you name?" "What colors are they?"

In the Child Care Settings study, children in centers spent their time in free-choice activities (25 percent) and adult-directed creative activities (23 percent), physical exercise (19 percent), and instruction (15 percent). Children in home care spent more time in free-choice activities (29 percent) and physical exercise (26 percent), less time in adult-directed creative activities (19 percent) and instruction (10 percent). The biggest difference observed was that in most centers children did not watch TV, whereas in almost all daycare homes they did.

Although there is immense variation among daycare centers, some differences can be predicted by knowing the type of center: franchised or independent, cooperative or commercial, and so on. Historically in the United States the largest suppliers of daycare have been private, nonprofit providers. Over the last twenty years, however, there has been a decline in the percent of nonprofit facilities and increase in for-profit facilities. Charitable organizations no longer have the money or the womanpower to invest in childcare.

As it turns out, whether a center is run for profit or not makes a significant difference in the kind of care it is likely to provide. Differences between for-profit and nonprofit centers are summarized in Table 2. Remembering that these are only averages, it is clear that for all counts on which there is a difference, and there is a difference on most, nonprofit daycare centers, especially those supported by public funds, come out ahead. They are more likely to have a trained and experienced staff, to offer a comprehensive program with a child-development component, and to adhere to a higher set of standards. The teachers are more likely to offer the children developmentally appropriate activities. The centers offer more services: screening, testing, immunization, transportation, social work, referral to other agencies or professionals. They pay their teachers higher wages. Although these average differences are not guarantees, they can be of some help in starting a search for the best

Table 2. Differences between Profit and Nonprofit Daycare Centers

Category	Profit	Nonprofit
Staff		
Training in child development	44%	66%
Education	14 years	14 years
Experience in daycare	5 years	4 years
Time in present center	2 years	3 years
Salaries	lower	higher
Parents		
Participation as volunteers	12%	45%
Decisions on policy	12%	61%
Children per caregiver		
Infants	4.5	3.5
Toddlers	7	5
Preschoolers	10	7
Overall quality		
Superior or good	16%	38%

Data from S. L. Kagan, "Examining Profit and Nonprofit Child Care: An Odyssey of Quality and Auspices," *Journal of Social Issues,* 47 (1991), 87–104; Whitebook et al., *Who Cares? Child Care Teachers and the Quality of Care in America.*

available daycare. Now let us look at some of the variations within the profit and nonprofit types of daycare.

For-Profit Centers

Currently about 40 percent of the daycare centers in the United States operate for profit. Some 2,000 of these are in daycare chains, such as the Kinder-Care Learning Centers, which now number over 1,200 in forty-odd states and take in an income of $200 million annually. But most for-profit centers are single-unit, "mom and pop" operations. Most offer full-day care. That care may be excellent, educational, individualized, and stimulating—or it may consist of custodial care in a baby warehouse. The level of quality in the center is very much linked to the state or county requirements for licensing. For-profit daycare centers do not have ratios and group sizes better than what the government requires, because to make a profit requires the largest possible number of children for each adult salary.

Independent centers. These are private daycare centers, often referred to as "proprietary centers," which are run for profit. About half of the centers in the United States are of this type. These centers have no eligibility criteria and will take anyone who can pay the fee, which is likely to be lower than some other kinds of daycare centers. Usually they are quite small, enrolling about thirty children, and often located in converted stores or shops. They are typically family-run operations, staffed by the owner and one or two assistants who are not professionally trained. Their clients tend to be homogeneous and from the neighborhood in which they are located. They have less recreational space and equipment and fewer educational activities than other daycare centers. They offer no social or health services. Parents do not usually participate in the program, simply dropping their children off in the morning and picking them up at night. Twenty-eight percent of the daycare centers in this country are independent for-profit centers.

Chains. These are also profit-making centers, but franchised or part of a chain. About 9 percent of daycare centers belong to commercial chains. Kinder-Care, Mary Moppet, and Children's World are examples of successful commercial ventures. There has been a dramatic rise in so-called Kentucky Fried daycare chains since 1970. Kinder-Care, for example, grew from 60 centers in 1974 to

280 in 1978 to 340 in 1979 to 1,100 in 1988. All the centers in a chain have uniform facilities and programs. Their main aim is cost effectiveness—children are "units" to be managed. Developing a model and then replicating or franchising it on a large scale apparently makes daycare a reasonable business undertaking.

So does paying staff the minimum wage. For-profit centers are most likely to cut corners on staff training, salaries, and benefits. Their staff turnover was the highest observed in any centers included in the Child Care Settings study. They also had the largest centers. On the average, these centers enroll seventy to one hundred children in classes of about twenty. They tend to be well equipped, located in new buildings, and offer nutritional food and some educational activities. They have colorful brochures and worksheets. They are likely to emphasize the quality of the physical facility over the quality of the staff. Their minimal staff-child ratios make them illegal in some states. Ratios of children to caregivers are higher in chains (approximately ten children per caregiver) than in any other kind of center, including independent for-profit centers (approximately eight children per caregiver).

Nonprofit Centers

Community and church centers. About 40 percent of the daycare centers in the United States are run by private community or charitable organizations, churches, or cooperating parents. Those run by community or church organizations are usually for children from poor families. They emphasize personal attention and affection from caregivers (who may be volunteers) rather than physical facilities. They are often located in old buildings, such as church or community halls, and have limited recreational facilities. They do not stress health care, social services, or education. About one third of all churches provide or allow some sort of daycare on their premises.

Company centers. In small numbers, corporations, factories, hospitals, universities, and trade unions have provided daycare as a fringe benefit for their employees. Usually the center is at a site near the company building, so that mothers can drop in to see their children during breaks. These centers are relatively large (eighty to one hundred children on the average), with well-qualified and well-paid staff. They are likely to offer the full range of services: education, recreation, and health care in bright, cheerful, and well-equipped physical settings. The characteristics of the company may carry over to the center. For example, hygiene may be particularly stressed in a hospital daycare center, or assembly-line routines—"All line up for juice now." "You powder, I'll pin!"—in a factory. But the high cost of setting up a center prohibits most companies from considering this employee benefit. Only 3,500 of the six million employers in America offer childcare assistance of *any* kind to their employees, and only about a thousand, most of them hospitals, actually have on-site daycare.

In a representative survey of 600 adults in American households with incomes over $25,000 in 1987, the overwhelming majority wanted their employers to be more involved in childcare. Only 5 percent of the employees surveyed had on-site daycare, but 70 percent of them said they wanted it, and 39 percent of them said they would consider changing jobs if they knew of a company that offered it. On the other hand, employees (and employers) who have on-site care are disillusioned. Most employees do not like it, and most employers find it too expensive to establish, too risky to operate, too complicated to administer, and too likely to be underused.

Cooperative centers. In private cooperative centers, parents do a major part of the care, maintenance, and decision making, usually with the guidance of a paid director and some teachers. Fees are lower as a result of this in-kind service, but cooperative centers usually attract high-income families because the parents must have some flexibility in their work schedules to fit in their time at the center. Problems may arise if parents disagree. These centers usually stress education and ideology rather than equipment, food, or health services.

Government centers. Only about 10 percent of the daycare centers in the United States receive government funding. These centers offer families the widest range of services, from meals to medical attention, from toys to transportation, and all meet standards to ensure adequate physical facilities, equipment, staff, and educational programs. There is usually an emphasis on children's cognitive development in an environment offering books, music, blocks, sand, paints, puzzles, lessons, and conversation. Eligibility is restricted to low-income families. The parents are often involved in policy making and may participate in auxiliary educational programs. The center staff may include student aides, community volunteers, and senior citizens as well as trained teachers and directors. The main goal is often preparing children for school. These programs include Head Start centers.

Research centers. This category includes only a tiny fraction of existing daycare centers, but it is a significant fraction because much of the research on daycare effects has been done here. These centers, usually affiliated with universities, reflect what is currently thought to be optimal daycare practice. The physical environment is spacious and stimulating. The educational curriculum is based on the latest in child-development research as well as tried and true traditional nursery-school activities. The focus is usually language and intellectual development. The staff is ample, experienced, and extensively trained in child development. The teachers meet regularly with the researchers to talk about the program and the children. Teachers also make an effort to talk regularly with the parents, who tend to be from low-income or university student families. Classes are small, and an effort is usually made to keep children with the same caregiver and classmates while they are in the program.

Part-Time Arrangements

Sometimes working mothers can adjust their schedules so that they need only part-time daycare; sometimes they use a combination of arrangements. In these cases, nursery schools and prekindergarten classes can serve as daycare settings.

Nursery schools. Private nursery schools tend to be for the relatively affluent. They were not originally designed to serve the needs of full-time working mothers, and most offer morning programs only. Recently, however, accompanying the increased need for daycare, there have been adjustments. Some nursery schools now offer an extended day (from 9:00 to 2:30 rather than 9:00 to noon); others have joined with day nurseries to offer combined services. Traditionally, nursery schools have been concerned with children's creative expression and social adjustment and have offered children an opportunity for enriched play as they choose freely from a lavish buffet of blocks, dolls, dressups, puzzles, books, paints, and pets, with assistance, advice, comfort, or instruction provided by the teacher as needed. In the last fifteen years many nursery schools have also shifted to a more developmental curriculum, rather than simply providing opportunities for free expression and exploration. Montessori nursery schools, which were always more oriented toward cognitive development, have also increased in popularity.

Daycare at school. Schools in all states now provide kindergarten for five-year-olds, and many are going in the direction of providing prekindergarten programs for four-year-olds. In 1987, twenty-four states were funding prekindergarten programs for four-year-olds. These state-funded programs are for disadvantaged children only, but eventually they may be available for all children. Many local school districts are currently operating prekindergarten programs for families other than those with low incomes. These are all part-day programs. Schools have also increased the availability of extended-day kindergartens—kindergartens that go to 1:00 or 2:00 in the afternoon. Although this is still not full-time daycare, it does have advantages. School programs employ more qualified teachers, with more training in early childhood education, than any other program. Teachers get the highest salaries and are least likely to leave their jobs. Preparing children for school is an important goal of these programs.

These, then, are the general types of daycare available in the United States today. They range from single in-home sitters to centers with five hundred children. I have tried to describe what goes on in each type of daycare, based on available research. But remember that these descriptions are based on averages. There is much variability in any particular type of care. There are daycare homes that provide outstanding care and daycare homes that should be closed down; there are daycare centers that make us wish we were three again and daycare centers that are not much better than kiddy jails. In the next chapter we begin to look at what effect being in daycare—in any of these forms—is likely to have on children.

5 / Effects on Children

Social scientists have been studying the effects of daycare on children for two decades now. Their usual method is to locate two groups of children—those attending daycare and those not attending daycare—and then to compare how well the two groups do on some test. If the average score on the test for the group of children in daycare is higher than the average score for the other, they conclude that daycare has a positive effect on development; if it is lower, then daycare is damaging. This kind of study is far too simple to do justice to the complex question of daycare effects. Consequently, although a consistent pattern does seem to emerge from the results of all the studies done so far, we should be aware of some of the limitations in this research.

First, only a limited number of daycare settings have been studied. Often they have been university-based, well-funded, and well-run centers that reflect what we think of as the best possible daycare. We don't know as much about the quality of the other centers studied because researchers have not usually observed and described children's experiences systematically there. One might assume that these centers would also be of better-than-average quality because the directors who agree to participate would be proud of their centers and would offer relatively good care. The evidence we have, however, suggests that in terms of their class sizes, adult-child ratios, and the likelihood that their caregivers have been trained in child development, the average quality of daycare in these studies is about the same as the average quality of daycare available nationwide.[1] It seems likely, then, that the results of the studies I will describe apply to the *majority* of daycare programs available today. Unfortunately, we do not know the effects of significantly worse-than-average daycare, in which a sizable number of children are placed. This is one important limitation on the research evidence to be presented.

A second limitation lies in the kinds of comparisons that researchers have made when they contrast daycare and nondaycare children. It is essential to make sure that the groups being compared are identical in every way except in the one thing being studied: being in daycare. Meeting this seemingly obvious condition has been a problem for researchers. For one thing, they do not always know much about the experiences of children who are not in daycare. Although these children are not attending daycare at the time of the study, they may have had daycare-like experiences in a playgroup, nursery school, or with a babysitter. This could reduce the differences between the two groups. For another thing, although the researcher can pick children for the two groups who are the same age, whose families have comparable incomes, and who live in the same neighborhood, it is not possible to rule out other differences between the families that choose to use daycare and those that don't. These differences would include such important factors as the mother's work status and the parents' attitudes toward employment. Ideally, in a scientific study, the researcher would assign one group of children to go to daycare and the other to stay at home *on a random basis.* But this has only been done in two studies of daycare,[2] using nonworking welfare mothers. It is unlikely that many parents would be willing to have their work status or their child's care determined by the random roll of a researcher's dice. Because families make their own choices about work and childcare, and thus "self-select" themselves into daycare or nondaycare groups, it is not possible to say with certainty that the differences observed between daycare and parent-care children are *caused* by daycare. There may also be something in the experiences these children have at home that would make them different.

A third limitation in assessing daycare effects comes from the lack of precision in our instruments for measuring children's development. Our tools for assessing differences are often quite primitive. There is no yardstick for precisely measuring children's social, emotional, and intellectual growth. We can make rough estimates, but these may miss subtle and important distinctions.

One tool used for getting such estimates, for example, is the standard intelligence test. In the preschool period, intelligence tests measure children's abilities to use and understand language (words, concepts, stories) and to manipulate and organize materials (putting pegs in holes, matching geometric figures, copying complex designs with blocks). The child's score on such a test can then be compared to national norms. This measure does tell us something important about how the child is progressing—in particular, by the time children are three or four years old, it gives a reasonably good prediction of how well they are likely to do in school. But it does not indicate anything about the child's earlier progress or about the development of social skills, emotions, creativity, or practical problem solving. Our measures of these qualities are more shaky. The research results to be dis-

cussed are thus limited to quite general and global estimates of children's mental and psychological development.

Nevertheless, despite these limitations in samples, designs, and measures, research does shed some light on
the question of how daycare is likely to affect children.

Physical Health and Development

Children's physical development is the least difficult aspect of development to assess. We can at least see and
agree on whether the child has a cold or can climb stairs.
A number of studies of daycare effects have included
reports from pediatricians, teachers, and mothers on
children's physical well-being and standard tests of
motor abilities (walking, jumping, throwing a ball, han-
dling tools) to find out whether children in daycare differ
in these ways from children who stay at home with their
mothers. The findings are quite consistent. For children
from poor families, daycare (in either university-based
or community facilities) advances motor development
and activity, increases height and weight faster, and de-
creases the likelihood of pediatric problems (from 50
percent to 23 percent, in one study).[3] For physical
growth, daycare centers and daycare homes both have
these advantages; for motor development, the benefit
occurs only in centers. This probably comes from the fact
that daycare centers offer better food, safety, health services, and opportunities for supervised exercise with lots
of space, equipment, and other children than what a
child would receive at home.

On the other hand, if children already come from
families and homes that provide these opportunities, no
benefit in physical development accrues from going to
even an excellent daycare center. There is no advantage

for middle-class children attending a daycare program in physical growth, activity, or motor skills.[4] There is, however, a difference in health. Children in daycare centers, whatever their family backgrounds, get more flu, rashes, colds, coughs, and ear infections than children at home.[5] They catch everything that is going around, even if they are from the best of homes and in good-quality daycare. Especially in centers, children who are in daycare get illnesses at younger ages.[6] In one study in a model daycare center, infants had ten respiratory illnesses in one year, whereas children who were at home had seven. By the time the children in the daycare center were two years old, however, they had made their way through the germs, and they experienced fewer respiratory illnesses than the children at home. By age five, children in the daycare center had only four colds a year; the children at home had twice as many.

This study is unusual. Usually comparative studies find that, overall, daycare children are sick more often than children at home. Partly this may be because most children in daycare are not enrolled in the same center with the same children for five years, so they are always encountering new germs. Partly it may be because most children in daycare are not in model centers. In ordinary daycare, children have two to four episodes of gastroenteritis per year, whereas children at home have only half that many. With conscientious handwashing, though, the incidence of stomach upsets in daycare children drops to almost the same level as in children at home. Handwashing and other hygienic measures, such as having different people prepare the food and diaper the children, also reduce the incidence of diarrhea and cytomegalovirus (CMV)—a virus that does not affect the children but can cause fetal damage if their mothers are pregnant.

Thus it seems that daycare offers opportunities for

motor development and physical growth that some children would not get at home. But it also offers exposure to germs and illnesses. The key to minimizing children's illnesses is to find a stable daycare facility in which caregivers follow strict procedures of physical hygiene.

Intellectual Development

A child's runny nose may be a price mothers are willing to pay to have their children in a daycare center while they work, especially if most of the nose wiping is done by daycare staff. But what about the child's intellectual growth? Is daycare detrimental to mental development, as some have feared? This has been the focus of over thirty different studies in the last two decades.

The good news from almost all these studies—in Canada, England, Sweden, Czechoslovakia, Bermuda, as well as the United States—is that care in a decent daycare facility has no apparent detrimental effects on children's intellectual development. Only two or three of these studies found that scores on tests of perception, language, and intelligence were lower for children attending a daycare center than for children of comparable family backgrounds being cared for by parents at home.[7] The children in these studies had been in daycare from an early age, and the centers they attended met only minimal standards. Adult-child ratios for two-year-olds in one study, for example, ranged from one adult for sixteen children to one adult for twenty-four children, and care was custodial at best. With these exceptions, studies have shown that children in daycare centers do at least as well as children at home, and often they do better.[8] This was true not only in daycare centers at Harvard University, the University of North Carolina, and Syracuse University, but also in community centers in New York, Chicago, Toronto, Boston, and Stockholm. Children in these centers were found to do better than children at home on tests of verbal fluency, memory, and comprehension; they were observed to copy designs with blocks, solve problems, string beads, write their names, and draw circles, squares, and triangles earlier than children at home. Their speech was more complex, and they were able to identify other people's feelings and points of view earlier. On IQ tests there may be a difference of as much as twenty to thirty points between daycare and parent-care groups. Mothers of children in centers corroborate these results, reporting that daycare teaches children things they wouldn't have learned at home—concepts, arithmetic, practical skills. (The only thing mothers complain about is that their children also pick up more bad language.[9])

This apparent advantage of daycare-center attendance occurs most often for children aged two to four years who are from poor families, although differences for middle-class children have also been observed in some studies. The gains in intellectual development increase for the first couple of years that the child is in the center, but daycare children do not typically stay ahead of nondaycare children. When nondaycare children get to kindergarten or first grade, they soon catch up to their daycare peers and differences between the groups diminish or disappear.[10] What daycare seems to do is to speed up children's intellectual development during the preschool period rather than to change it permanently.

The same kinds of results have been obtained in studies of differences between children who go to nursery schools and those who do not.[11] At the beginning of kindergarten or first grade, children from middle-class families who have been to nursery school are better able to manage on their own, know more about their environment, ask more questions; they are more ingenious with materials, have richer vocabularies, are more verbally expressive. Their conversations are more "connected." Their play is more purposeful, persistent, and creative; they do more school-related activities, including writing. Their peers as well as their teachers think they have better ideas and do better work. Similar differences in intellectual performance have been observed for poor children who attend model preschool programs.[12] Thus it seems that participation in a preschool program, daycare center, or nursery school, even part time, can have at least temporary benefits for a child's intellectual development.

But the same acceleration has usually not been observed for children in daycare homes or with babysitters. Although some studies have found no significant differences between children in daycare homes and daycare centers, when there is a difference in intellectual development it favors children in center daycare over those in home daycare. Children with a home provider or babysitter, it seems, do about the same as children at home with their mothers, while children in centers may do better.[13] In the New York Infant Day Care Study, for example, a study of some 400 children from lower-income families attending 11 community daycare centers and 100 daycare homes, of which most were in supervised daycare networks, children in centers and homes started off at six to twelve months getting about the same scores on standard intelligence tests.[14] They stayed at the same level through their second year, but by three years of age the scores of children in daycare homes had dropped to a significantly lower level than those of children in centers, and were at the same level as those of children at home with parents.

In the Chicago Study of Childcare and Development,

my students and I looked at 150 two- to four-year-old children from a mixture of home backgrounds and a variety of care arrangements, including home with parents or babysitters, in daycare homes, in nursery schools, in daycare centers, and in combined nursery school/babysitter arrangements.[15] All of these childcare arrangements occurred naturally in the community; they were not exceptionally good or model facilities. The children were tested on their ability to understand sentences, to name colors, fruits, and animals, to remember numbers, to identify photographs of objects, to use play materials, to solve problems, to label pictures of emotions, to copy designs made with blocks, to visualize how things would look to another person, and to communicate a message. On all these measures of intellectual competence, a clear difference was found between children in home care and in center care. The children in centers were, on the average, six to nine months advanced over children cared for at home by their mothers or babysitters or in daycare homes. The differences appeared for children of all family backgrounds, for both boys and girls, after as little as six months in daycare.

In sum, it appears likely that there is something about daycare centers and nursery schools that stimulates or maintains children's intellectual development, at least until the beginning of school. Although differences were not observed in every study, when differences were observed they were consistently in the direction of advanced development for daycare children.

Yet it must be emphasized that these findings do not mean that all children will benefit from being in daycare. The daycare centers that had these apparent advantages, though not all exceptional, were all of relatively good quality; poor-quality centers would not be expected to have positive outcomes. The children most likely to benefit from daycare centers came from relatively poor families; children from affluent families did not gain so much. The measures of intellectual development used were of an academically oriented sort: language skills, manipulative abilities, perceptual abilities. Children from homes might do better than children in centers on tests of a more practical sort (buying a loaf of bread, getting to the store). Although centers in these studies were superior to homes for supporting children's intellectual development, this does not mean that the same kinds of benefit might not be possible in homes; these studies all dealt with averages, not individual facilities or children. Some children might do better in a home setting than they would in a center; some homes undoubtedly provide more intellectual stimulation than many centers. Differences between children in daycare centers and daycare homes are less. when the daycare homes are of high quality. For example, in one study, although the competence of children in *unlicensed* daycare homes was inferior to that of children in centers, the competence of children in *regulated* homes was equivalent.[16] More telling, in another study, when care in daycare homes was enriched by the experimental addition of an educational curriculum, the intellectual performance of the children was observed to improve to the level of children in daycare centers.[17]

Social Relations and Social Competence

Over the preschool years, as they are learning to count and color, to play and paint, children also grow in social skills and develop relationships. They progress in interacting with their peers from simply staring to approaching and exploring, to smiling and offering toys, to interactions that are intense and reciprocal. They learn to play complex games, to act out roles, and to participate in cooperative activities in groups. They make friends and acquire enemies. A large number of researchers have focused on daycare children's relations with their peers, expecting that since these children have so much more experience with other children, this must make a difference in their social relations with agemates. They have observed children in their daycare settings as they interact with other children after greater or lesser amounts of time in daycare. They have brought unacquainted pairs of children who are in either daycare or parental care into a set-up play situation in the laboratory and watched their interactions. They have tested children from different care arrangements on their willingness to cooperate and help one another. The results of their studies suggest that daycare also makes a difference in peer relations.[18]

Although daycare and parent-care children do not differ in the kinds of interactions they have with familiar friends or playmates, daycare children are more at ease socially when they meet a new child. In unfamiliar situations, children attending daycare centers or nursery schools are more outgoing, less timid and fearful, more helpful and cooperative than children who spend their time at home. They are more likely to share materials and behave empathically toward other children. Their interactions with peers are also more complex and mature. They can sustain their play longer and respond more appropriately and immediately to the other children's behavior.

Over the preschool years, children also become more socially competent with adults. They learn how to cooperate, to be polite, to behave in public. They learn how to do things on their own without constant adult help and supervision. They learn to take care of themselves, to make decisions, and to follow through on them. Researchers have studied how children differ in these respects as well. Their results reveal that in these ways too there are differences between children who attend daycare and those who do not.[19]

Daycare children, they have found, are more self-confident, assured, and assertive in unfamiliar test situations. They act more at ease and are more likely to admit to an examiner that they don't know the answer to a test question. They are more likely to talk to researchers who are studying them. They can more competently show a stranger around their home, get her a glass of water, and show her their toys. They tend to be liked better by adults who are meeting them for the first time. Daycare children are also self-sufficient and independent of adults. They can make their own choices, dress themselves, and brush their hair at younger ages. Yet they are more cooperative and helpful to parents, teachers, or examiners when the situation requires it. They are more verbally expressive and knowledgeable about the social world—for example, knowing what activities and toys that boys and girls prefer. When playing with toys, they act in less stereotyped and more original ways. They don't just play with toy trucks as vehicles, for instance, but find original uses for them—such as doing laundry in the back. They know more about social and moral rules—for example, that it is worse to hit another child than it is to talk when the teacher is talking. When they start school, children who have attended daycare or nursery school are better adjusted, more persistent at their tasks, and more likely to be leaders.

Like the differences in intellectual competence, these differences in social competence do not appear in all studies of all daycare programs for all children, but when differences do appear, children in daycare are on average more advanced. As with the differences in intellectual development, the differences have been observed more often for children in daycare centers and nursery schools than for children in daycare homes or with babysitters. In one study in which mothers were interviewed, increased self-reliance by their children as a result of daycare experience was mentioned by 60 percent of the mothers with children in daycare centers, 50 percent of the mothers with children in daycare homes, and 11 percent of the mothers whose children were with babysitters.[20]

Considering the results of all these studies, then, it looks as if daycare (at least the daycare that has been studied) promotes or at least does not hinder children's social development. But there is another side to the story. The same studies also show that children in daycare, in addition to having these positive qualities, are sometimes less polite, less agreeable, less compliant with their mother's or caregiver's demands and requests, less respectful of others' rights, more irritable and more rebellious, more likely to use profane language, more boisterous, more competitive and aggressive with their peers than children who have not been in daycare.[21] In one recent study of 600 children about to enter kindergarten, John Bates and his associates found that boys who attended daycare full time from the time they were one till they were three years old were more aggressive than those who did not attend daycare.[22] In another large study of 835 kindergarten children, Kathy Thornburg and her colleagues found that children who attended daycare, even part time, during the preschool years were more aggressive toward their peers and less compliant with adults than children who spent the entire period at home.[23] And in yet a third new study, Alice Honig found that preschoolers who had been in full-time daycare starting any time in the first three years were more aggressive and disobedient than preschoolers who had not had this daycare experience.[24]

These differences in aggressive and noncompliant behavior, though not inevitable, appear in tests and in natural observations, in the daycare center and on the playground, with adults and with other children, with strangers and with parents, for children from model and mediocre daycare programs. They are more marked for boys and for children from lower-income families, but they also appear for girls and middle-class children.

The problem obviously is how to interpret these differences. Are daycare children more socially competent or less? They are helpful but also demanding; cooperative but bossy; friendly but aggressive; outgoing but rude. My interpretation is that in the preschool years daycare children as a group are more developmentally advanced in the social realm, just as they are in the intellectual realm, and that is why they are more knowledgeable, self-sufficient, and able to cooperate. But they are also more independent and determined to get their own way, and they do not always have the social skills to achieve this smoothly—which is why they are more aggressive, irritable, and noncompliant.

Others have claimed that the aggression and noncompliance observed in daycare children reflects psychological maladjustment.[25] They suggest that daycare places children at risk for developing emotional problems. There are several reasons to question this interpretation. First, although daycare children are more aggressive on the playground, they are not generally considered by their teachers to be unlikable or difficult to manage.[26] Second, when characteristics of the child and of the family are taken into account, the apparent differences in children's aggression decrease dramatically.[27] Third, when a curriculum that focuses on teaching children social skills is implemented in the daycare center, the heightened aggression of daycare children is eliminated.[28] And fourth, although daycare children are more aggressive from preschool through first or second grade, they are not more aggressive in the later school years.[29]

As we saw for differences in intellectual development, differences in social behavior—both positive and negative—between children in daycare and children at home seem to carry over into the first few school grades, but then decrease and largely disappear. Because they are not permanent, all these differences might be better thought of as differences in children's performance rather than differences in their competence, as the result of differences in learning rather than differences in development. Attending daycare or nursery school speeds up children's development rather than changing it in a basic way. All children learn their letters, we know, but children in daycare programs do it earlier. All children are eventually able to leave their mother's side to explore a new environment, but children in daycare do it at younger ages. All children get over their inhibition with strangers; daycare children do it faster. All children learn to cooperate with their peers; daycare children learn it sooner. Daycare children enter the world outside the home when they are younger, and their experiences in that outside world lead to new skills. More than simply learning new skills, in fact, what children in daycare learn is a different "culture." It is a culture that is as different from the culture of being at home with mother as the Anglo culture is different from the Latino, the French from the English. They learn a culture of interacting with groups of people, of dealing with newcomers and friends who go away, of figuring out institutional rules, of achieving academic success, of making decisions about what to do without mother's advice. Young children who stay home during the preschool years do not enter this culture until they get to school.

6/ Places, Programs, Peers

Just how is the "culture" of daycare different from that of home care? Why do children's experiences in the daycare culture seem to accelerate their growing independence, knowledge, and social competence? What is it about particular daycare settings that leads to children's learning new skills? In this chapter we will look at three different aspects of the daycare culture that affect children's experiences and learning: the physical space and equipment, the educational program or curriculum, and the presence of other children.

Places

What children remember most about daycare years later, researchers have discovered, is the physical experience—the discomfort of lying quietly on their backs at naptime, of not being able to get a swing, of digging in the sand, or eating outdoors on the grass.[1] The experience of daycare is a sensual one, and we might expect that differences in the physical setting would affect how children behave and what they learn in different daycare programs. Certainly the physical setting of daycare centers is dramatically different from a home environment, and this may be part of the reason we find differences in children's development in these two types of care.

Space. Researchers have investigated the effects of variation in space, equipment, and materials in daycare settings in an attempt to find out how children's behavior and development are influenced by the physical setting. Space, it turns out, is related both to the size of the classroom and to the number of children in the class. The usual measure of space researchers use, therefore, is not simply the total space in the setting but the space per child. Several researchers have set up experimental playgroups in different-sized classrooms, allowing, for example, 15, 25, 50, or 75 square feet per child. When the space per child is very limited (less than 25 square feet), the studies show, children become more physical and aggressive with their peers, more destructive with their toys; they spend more time climbing or doing nothing, and less time running, jumping, chasing, and interacting socially.[2] In the United States, licensing standards for daycare centers and daycare homes ensure space that exceeds this limit of crowding (more than 35 square feet per child). Thus space is probably not a major influence on the development of children in most daycare settings, at least in those that meet licensing requirements.[3]

What may be more important is the way that space is organized. An organization that allows children privacy and quiet, where different kinds of activities—loud block play and quiet puzzle play, or messy finger painting and neat pine-cone collecting—are kept clearly separated, may be more beneficial than simply more square feet of play area.[4]

Materials. The materials that go into the separate activity areas can also be important. Different kinds of behavior obviously are typical for different play areas. Outdoors, with playground equipment, children do more running, playing, laughing, rough and tumble; they are less aggressive, more mature, cooperative, and sociable; they talk more to peers than to teachers and play lengthy, complex games. Indoors, in the dramatic play area (dressups and dolls), children also talk among themselves and have complex social interactions. In the building-construction area (blocks and boards), they talk less—except for quarrels—but their play is complex, rich, and challenging. In the art and academic areas (paints and puzzles), their play is complex and they use the materials constructively, but involvement with these materials is more likely to be accompanied by interaction with the teacher than is involvement with blocks, boards, dolls, or dressups. With materials for "messing around" (sand, clay, buttons, assorted junk), their activities, often with other children, are creative and experimental but somewhat less complex. Small toys also bring out less complex behaviors as children do what the toys suggest: with toy guns they behave aggressively; with checkers and pickup sticks they interact socially; with gyroscopes and microscopes they play alone. If there are no materials available and the equipment is fixed, inflexible, or limited, children spend their time watching, waiting, cruising, touching, imitating, chatting, quarreling, and horsing around with peers; their play is of low complexity and intellectual value. All children do better in centers with toys and materials that are varied and educational.[5]

The complexity and intensity of children's involvement with materials is also influenced by the number of activities each play area offers. Good play areas have four or five things for each child to do. For example, in the sandbox there is not only sand, but shovels, pails, water, and a dump truck; the doll corner has not only dolls but doll clothes, furniture, and a house. A more plentiful supply of materials leads to more cooperative, constructive, and relevant participation and less conflict.[6]

Overall quality. Space of good physical quality can be found in homes or centers, although materials that elicit high-level constructive play (puzzles, blocks, art) may be more likely in centers, with opportunities for free play and tactile exploration (water, sand, dough, pillows) more likely in homes. In either setting, the quality of the physical space affects the adults' behavior as well as the children's. In daycare settings where the physical equipment and space are varied, accessible, complex, and offer children lots to do and lots of choices, not only are children more involved but caregivers are more sensitive, friendly, and interactive.[7] It is this combination of good materials and space and responsive caregiver behavior that is the best predictor of positive outcomes for children. Just having more numerous or more exotic toys and playthings in a home or center does not guarantee developmental gains.[8] In one study, cameras, puppets, and tape recorders were added to four-year-olds' daycare classes—with no apparent effects on the children's intellectual development. If their teachers had been trained in how to best utilize these materials, and had interacted with the children using them in these ways, some benefits might have occurred. In physical settings of good quality, caregivers can both allow children freedom to explore and spend their time demonstrating constructive activities with the materials available, rather than supervising and scolding all the time.

Programs

An educational curriculum is another critical factor that distinguishes homes and daycare centers. Although certainly many daycare centers are merely custodial and many homes offer children a rich diet of intellectual and social stimulation, for the most part it is only centers that offer children *formal* educational activities. These vary widely in type and content from center to center, however. What kind of influence do educational activities have, and how do children's experiences differ depending on what the center provides?

Open and closed. In one kind of daycare center or nursery school, the teacher is controlling, directive, and didactic. She tells the children what to do and when to do it. She gives the children explicit lessons, according to a strict schedule. This program has been called by various names: "structured," "closed," "formal." At the other extreme are centers where the teacher is unintrusive and indirect. She prepares materials and activities for the children but then lets them choose among them, going at their own pace, following their own interests, and making discoveries about the social and physical world on their own. She guides, encourages, and helps the children in their activities but does not exhort, direct, instruct, or restrict. This kind of program has been called, in contrast to the first, "unstructured," "open," "informal."

In a closed program, the teacher controls what happens and ensures that what is intended actually occurs. She makes clear to the children (and often their parents) her goals and expectations about what is right for the child to do. Her behavior is consistent and predictable. An open program may be more chaotic because the teacher is not in direct control. Her behavior and that of the children are more variable. Closed programs provide clear limits and structured instruction, but lack opportunities for children to behave independently, to act on their own initiative, to have informal, spontaneous, one-to-one interactions with the teacher or other children.

Open programs offer varied activities, opportunities for rewarding contact with peers, freedom to explore, and the chance to make choices and decisions; adult input and engagement are low.

As might be expected, these two kinds of programs have distinctly different effects on children's behavior. A number of studies have compared children in open and closed programs in preschool classes and the primary grades.[9] In closed programs, children show less independence, less cooperation, less initiative, less helping, less imaginative play, less play with peers, less physical activity, and less aggression; their activities are more purposeful and task-oriented. In open classes, children do more functional and imaginative play with peers, more independent work, more work and helping with another child; they are more likely to persist on a task, talk about it, and ask questions. The two kinds of program are reflected not only in children's behavior in the classroom itself but in their performance on tests outside the classroom. Children in closed programs do better on intelligence and achievement tests; children in open programs do better on tests of curiosity, inventiveness, and problem solving.

In the real world, programs are seldom one extreme or the other; most are somewhere in between. They offer some prescribed, structured activities or lessons at some time during the day, but also give children opportunities for free play and free choice. This balance between structured activities and free choice is important. In one study of nursery school programs in Great Britain and the United States by Kathy Sylva and her colleagues, programs offering a *moderate* number of structured activities were found to be ideal.[10] In programs with just two structured educational activities per half-day session, children were observed to play constructively with the prescribed task materials even after the structured activity was completed. Their play was more elaborate and included more complex, cognitively worthwhile and challenging actions (such as building, drawing, doing puzzles) than that of children in either more closed programs with a greater number of prescribed lessons and tasks or more open programs with no prescribed activities. Assigning children tasks, these investigators concluded, can promote children's concentration and imagination by helping them sustain attention and master new skills. It can also, if taken to an extreme, become too restricting. Their recommendation for an optimal curriculum is "a basic diet of free choice punctuated lightly by prescribed educational tasks."

Teachers agree,[11] and so do the results of other studies.[12] Children in classes with the greatest number of structured activities have low gains in cognitive abilities; children in classes with no structured activities have low gains in creativity and achievement. With moderate structure and some room for children to initiate their own activities, children gain in cognition, achievement, and creativity; their self-esteem also tends to be higher.

The degree of structure in a program is usually combined with another dimension, the educational content of the program. Closed programs are more likely to focus on academic content; they are likely to emphasize language, prereading, manipulation of objects, and other intellectual skills. Open programs are more likely to give priority to children's enjoyment, self-expression, creativity, and sociability. Again, most programs are somewhere in between these two extremes—happily so, because children need both kinds of content to develop into well-rounded individuals.

Combinations. Researchers have asked how much difference it makes just where a daycare program falls on these two related dimensions. In one major study of pre-school programs, researchers Louise Miller and Jean Dyer compared the effects of programs that differed in the amount of structure and the content of the curriculum. They set up a number of model preschool programs in four different schools that were attended by children from low-income families.[13] Then they observed the behavior of teachers and children in these programs and tested the children's abilities throughout the school term and three years later.

The direct instruction program they set up (modeled after the Distar curriculum of Sigfried Engelmann, Carl Bereiter, and Wesley Becker) was highly structured and totally academic. Every day a teacher directed young-sters in small groups of five or six in three twenty-minute lessons on reading, language, and arithmetic. The lessons were controlled completely by the teacher, according to a script she was given by the program designers. She modeled, corrected, and rewarded children's responses in a fast-paced, loud, repetitive drill of short questions and answers:

Teacher: This is a *wheel* (shows picture).

Child: Wheel.

Teacher: Good. It is a wheel. Let's all say it. This is a wheel.

Children: This is a wheel.

Teacher: Again.

Children: This is a wheel.

Teacher: Let's say it one more time . . .

Children in this direct instruction program gained more rapidly on tests of intelligence, and by the end of the preschool year they scored higher than children in any other program on arithmetic, sentence production, vocabulary, and persistence in a difficult task. Three years later, however, at the end of second grade in a non-Distar class, these children scored low on tests of IQ, letters, numbers, word meaning, inventiveness, and curiosity. Their preschool gains had completely disappeared. Even years later, in elementary and high school, children who had attended this kind of strictly structured program were less socially skilled and less academically oriented.

Another structured, academically oriented program set up in this study was modeled after the Demonstration and Research Center for Early Education (DARCEE) program in Nashville, Tennessee. This was a program designed to improve children's language skills and attitudes toward school. Like the Distar curriculum, it included intensive teacher instruction, small groups, and formal academic lessons. But the lessons were not simply repetitions of verbal patterns, as in the Distar program; they included playing table games, copying designs, and identifying letters and numbers. There were both formal and informal conversations between children and teachers, often one to one, and children were given free choices as well as prescribed lessons. This program was only moderately structured. In the tests, children in the DARCEE programs also gained rapidly on IQ tests—they had the highest scores of any group after eight weeks—and on tests of arithmetic, vocabulary, sentence production, and persistence, but, unlike the children in the Distar program, they also gained in curiosity, inventiveness, and social participation. Unlike the highly structured and academic Distar program, then, the moderately structured and more comprehensive DARCEE program had positive social-emotional outcomes as well as intellectual ones. What is more, the children in the DARCEE program continued to score high on tests of IQ, inventiveness, curiosity, and verbal-social skills at the end of the second grade.

In the model Montessori program set up by Miller and Dyer, as in all Montessori programs, the materials were structured but the schedule was open. Children were free to select whatever materials interested them and to work on them at their own pace, with little teacher interference. The teacher introduced the materials at what she thought were appropriate times, and kept records of children's use and progress with the materials, but gave no lessons in how to use them. Montessori materials themselves are "self-correcting." There is only one right way to build a tower with the Montessori graduated cylinders or to make the staircase with the pink blocks, for example. The content emphasized by the Montessori program is intellectual (prereading, sensory discrimination, concepts of size and weight). In the standard tests, children in this program excelled in curiosity and inventiveness at the end of the program school year, but three years later they were not only high in these qualities but also high in IQ, reading, and mathematics and were more highly motivated to achieve in school. Again, the benefits of another moderately structured program were demonstrated.

The most open and also the most socially oriented program in Miller's and Dyer's study was the so-called traditional nursery school. This program was child-centered and slow-paced. Most of the time children engaged in free play, choosing from make-believe, dressups, physical activities, puzzles, books, and science materials. At other times they had group activities such as singing, stories, and field trips. The teachers exerted no pressure; they were warm and accepting; the children were free to do whatever interested them. The goal of the program was happy children who were curious, self-motivated, and sociable. At the end of a year in this program, the children met the goals of the program; they had more curiosity and were more active socially. But they were also more aggressive and not as likely to do well in intelligence tests. Three years later, they were still high on verbal-social skills such as cooperation and initiating conversations but, as earlier, low in academic achievement.

In sum, the results of studies comparing different kinds of educational programs in daycare centers and nursery schools are consistent in pointing up the benefits—for constructive activity, for learning academic skills, for later achievement in school, for positive motivation and persistence, for problem solving, and for acquiring social skills—of programs that blend prescribed educational activities with opportunities for free choice, that have some structure but also allow children to explore a rich environment of objects and peers on their own without teacher direction, that include both academic and social activities.

The blending of academic and social content is particularly important for promoting children's social development. There are many programs available today—Montessori, Piagetian, Distar, behavioral—that promote children's academic knowledge, at least temporarily. But fewer focus on developing their social skills. Commonly, daycare and nursery teachers encourage children's self-direction and independence, self-expression and intellectual skills. In these programs, children are likely to be self-confident and outgoing, knowledgeable about words and clever about things—but they may also be more aggressive with their playmates. In one study, for example, children attending a model university-based program that focused on promoting children's intellectual development and independence were observed to be much better at taking intelligence tests but thirteen times more aggressive with other children on the playground when they got to first grade.[14] Children who develop social skills in daycare, who learn nonaggressive strategies for solving social problems, apparently do not pick these skills up while simply being around other children in a benign and permissive environment building with blocks, or while being given lessons in the ABC's. Social skills are learned only in daycare programs in which special efforts are made to teach them. In the most satisfactory daycare, it appears, children are offered a balanced menu of academic and social lessons.

Peers

Of course it would be impossible to offer children social lessons in daycare were it not for the presence of other children. This is a critical feature of the daycare culture. One reason, in fact, that many parents decide to send their children to daycare or nursery school is for the experience the children will gain from playing with others their own age. These parents hope and expect that the children will become more socially skilled, will learn to share, cooperate, make friends, compete without being aggressive, and perhaps learn more mature behaviors from their peers. Given the availability of other children in daycare centers and nursery schools, their hope is not unreasonable. But as I have already mentioned, the result of being with a group of other children is not so simple. Just having the opportunity to play with peers does not guarantee that the child will become empathic and cooperative and able to settle conflicts without coming to blows. Teaching children how to solve social problems is also necessary. But what is the ideal classroom composition for such teaching? Is experience with a single playmate best? Is experience with more children better? Is playing with many different kinds of children valuable?

One good friend. Studies have shown that when young children are playing with a familiar playmate (as opposed to playing with a child they have never met before), their play is more interactive, cooperative, and connected. The two children stay closer together, smile, imitate, and share more; they cry, fuss, and take away each other's toys less.[15] This observation suggests that having experience with even one other child might benefit children by giving them the opportunity to practice the more advanced social skills that occur only with friends. A study by Jacqueline Becker with very young children (only nine months old) tested whether the highly skilled interactions developed with a friend would generalize to an unfamiliar peer.[16] Pairs of first-born infants were brought together for ten one-hour play sessions in one of the children's homes. As the two children became friends, the frequency, complexity, and responsiveness of their interaction increased. On the eleventh visit, an unfamiliar child of the same age, who had not participated in this experience with a peer, came to visit. What happened showed that children who had had the experience of playing with another child did generalize their social skills to the new child. They were more sociable and responsive, sustained interactions longer, and initiated more games with the newcomer than did the inexperienced children. Another study, with older preschool children, showed the same result.[17] Having a regular playmate was associated with more responsive and lengthy interactions with a peer stranger. So it seems that repeated opportunities to play with one other child may be of value for the development of early social competence.

The same may be true for intellectual development. Play between pairs of children, researchers have observed, is more intellectually worthwhile and cognitively challenging than playing alone. Peers can serve as models and tutors, as well as competitive partners and congenial and cooperative playmates. Only children do certain things together, such as using the teeter-totter, playing with a jack-in-the-box, jumping off a platform twenty times, or playing peek-a-boo under a blanket. When children are playing with another child, their behavior is more complex than when they are playing by themselves.[18] Thus having the chance to play with another child is necessary for social development and good for intellectual development.

Peer interaction: how much with how many? In daycare settings, though, children do not usually just play with one other child; they play with many. In the Chicago Study of Childcare and Development, for example, we found that children in daycare centers and nursery schools played with an average of ten different children during a two-hour period, whereas children at home played with only two or three. Does playing with more children have any benefits for children's development beyond the benefits of playing with one other child?

In the Chicago study, children in larger classes knew more about social rules and expressions and were less shy with unfamiliar peers and adults. The more different children they played with, the more advanced were their intellectual abilities and social competence. But does this mean that the more children a child plays with the better? Probably not. For one thing, we do not know that playing with more children *caused* the children's advanced development. It may be that more advanced children sought out or attracted more children to play with.

For another thing, there are likely to be limits to how many children one can play with, limits that were not exceeded in the centers in our study. In the National Day Care Study, a massive study of 64 daycare centers and more than 3,000 children in Atlanta, Detroit, and Seattle, researchers found that children in large classes of more than twenty children did more poorly on tests and in the classroom than those in smaller groups.[19] In large classes children spent more time crying, acting hostile, or looking bored; they spent less time in activities that involved conversation, cooperation, reflection, innovation, and elaborate play. This finding has been supported in other studies too, where class size has varied.[20] It seems that there is a top limit beyond which detrimental effects are likely to occur.

With too many children per adult, it has been found, there are detrimental effects as well. There is less caregiver-child contact of any kind; children spend more of their time playing with other children, in active physical games or make-believe; they spend less time in intellectual activities (elaborated play, art, construction, work on puzzles); fewer of their questions are answered; their conversations are shorter; and contact with the caregiver is more likely to involve prohibitions, commands, corrections, and routines. With too many children for one adult to attend to, children suffer and so do the adults—who are worn out before the end of the day.[21]

The reason that children in larger classes spend their time crying and hitting rather than playing and thinking, however, is not just that there are more children around to interact with. It is also the result of the demands these other children place on the caregiver. When there are many children to care for, caregivers have less time for each child and their care is less sensitive and developmentally appropriate.[22] And even if the ratio of caregivers to children is the same because there are two or three caregivers in the class, the higher noise level and increased hubbub of a larger class can be more physically and psychologically demanding for both teachers and children. Thus, even though it may be valuable for the child to play with a number of other children, this does not mean that being in larger groups is better. Large classes allow children the opportunity to interact with more different playmates, but they also deprive them of teacher attention, guidance, and responsiveness. When children spend more of their time in daycare just watching, playing around with, fighting, and imitating other children, especially younger children, they tend to be less competent, socially and intellectually.[23] A happy medium of a moderate number of other children with whom to play and a caregiver who can give individual attention to each of them would seem to be ideal.

Variety of peers: mix or match? Children in daycare, as well as interacting with a larger number of children, also interact with a greater variety of different kinds of children than do children at home. This aspect of the daycare culture also may affect children's learning and relationships. In the Chicago study, for example, children with advanced social and cognitive abilities interacted with more diverse kinds of people—of different socioeconomic and ethnic groups, ages, and sexes.

Among the kinds of variety in children's playmates that researchers have studied, the two most common are gender and age. They have observed that children act differently in same-sex or same-age and mixed-sex or mixed-age playgroups. When boys and girls are included in coeducational groups in nursery school, for example, girls have been observed to be more independent and boys have been observed to be more socially responsive and less disruptive than when they are in same-sex groups.[24] For both boys and girls, then, the behavior exhibited in the mixed-sex groups is more competent than the behavior exhibited in the same-sex groups. In mixed-age groups as well, children are observed to be more socially competent. They have more frequent and complex interactions with their peers and are more cooperative, persistent, flexible, and knowledgeable in tests of social competence and intelligence. The advantage is especially marked for the younger children in the mixed-age group.[25]

Here again, though, there are probably limits to the advantages of interacting with a variety of other children. The mixed-age groups studied did not include a wide range of ages but a range of only two or three years. Including both one-year-olds and four-year-olds in a daycare group would not necessarily increase children's opportunities to learn. In daycare homes in fact, where age ranges are greater, it was observed in the National Day Care Home Study that mixed-age groups were not advantageous. For toddlers in mixed-age groups (with either infants or preschoolers), more time was spent alone, not interacting with either the caregiver or the other children; for preschoolers, if younger children were present, although more time was spent playing with the other children, less time was spent in stimulating interaction with the caregiver. What seemed best in a home daycare situation was a relatively narrow age range of not more than two years.

The issue of the influence of peers is thus a complex one. Experience with one other peer seems to be better than experience with none; experience with more different peers is probably better than experience with one; experience with too many peers in the same class or at the same time may be detrimental. Experience with a variety of other people appears to be enriching, but with too much diversity the advantage may be lost.

What happens within the daycare setting, including the child's experience with peers, however, depends to a large extent on the last critical feature of the daycare culture: the daycare provider. The contribution of the care provider underlies the effects of all the aspects of daycare we have discussed so far. The caregiver arranges the physical space and selects the equipment and materials, selects and administers the educational curriculum, divides the children into groups and supervises their social interaction. The caregiver is the stage manager of the daycare culture.

7 / Caregivers

Adult caregivers have many roles as they care for children. They minister to a child's body, mind, and soul. They provide education, stimulation, affection, and fun; they manage and discipline. In this chapter we discuss how caregivers—both in daycare and at home—foster children's development.

Daycare Providers

Multiple roles. One important role of the daycare provider is that of teacher. In the previous chapter we saw that the caregiver's teaching style significantly affects a child's behavior and development. When caregivers in daycare are actively involved in teaching children and providing them with interesting materials and a moderate number of educational tasks, this has clear benefits for the child's intellectual learning and achievement. If the content of the caregiver's lessons includes social as well as intellectual skills, then children's cooperation and social behavior with peers may also be enhanced. Thus caregivers in daycare can serve as teachers—and they often see this as their role. In the Child Care Settings study, one fifth of the center directors interviewed said that their main goal was to promote children's development; another 13 percent (mostly in Head Start or school-based programs) said it was to prepare children for school.

Another role daycare providers play is that of facilitator. The caregiver responds to children's needs and wishes and helps them to achieve their own ends. The need for people to respond to children's desires, interests, and expressions starts early in life. It is important for babies to learn that the world is a predictable place and that they can anticipate and to some extent control the people and things in it. To help infants develop this expectation, it is critical that caregivers interact with them not only frequently but in response to specific signals and demands. Knowing that when they cry someone comes to comfort or feed them, when they smile someone smiles back, when they reach for a toy out of their grasp someone gives it to them, encourages children to explore new situations and new people and promotes their development and confidence. When daycare providers are responsive to children's interests, goals, requests, and questions, the children are more independent, cooperative, and sociable.

Daycare providers also may see it as part of their role to provide children with love and affection. In the Child Care Settings study, the main goal of the majority of caregivers, both home providers and center directors, was to provide the children with a warm, loving environment. This is all for the good. If teachers create a negative emotional climate in their classrooms, children learn less. On the other hand, if teachers are too physically affectionate, it may distract children from their "work" and they will learn less. Caregivers who are overly warm and affectionate may foster children's sociability, happiness, and helpfulness—but they may not be so effective at teaching. To educate children demands more than a steady diet of hugs and kisses.

Nor is affection alone an effective way of getting children to do things they would rather not—and getting children to do things they would rather not is another part of the daycare provider's role. Caregivers must manage the children while they are at daycare and get them to behave. Daycare culture would be daycare chaos if caregivers were not clearly in charge. Daycare providers thus must not only be teachers and facilitators and creators of positive emotional climates; they must also be disciplinarians.

Praise is one way caregivers try to discipline or manage the children. Praise can be used effectively to manipulate children's behavior in the daycare setting. If children get consistently praised, researchers have demonstrated, they will stay close to the caregiver and interact with her. They will play with a child they would ordinarily ignore if the teacher praises them for that action. They will be more cooperative or more competitive, depending on what the caregiver praises. They will play with dolls rather than trucks if the caregiver rewards them for doing so. They will persist longer at a particularly difficult task they have been praised for working at. It is not simply the frequency of saying nice things to children that matters, but the frequency with which the caregiver praises the specific kinds of behavior she wants to see more of. When teachers simply go around being nice all the time no matter what the children are doing, children do not learn and achieve. When caregivers do not expect children to behave in particular ways—cooperative, assertive, persistent, quiet, polite—and do not consistently encourage them to act these ways and praise them for doing so, children are unlikely to learn these kinds of behavior.

It is even worse, though, if teachers go around constantly criticizing the children. Neither unconditional acceptance and permissiveness nor heavy-handed restriction and criticism are effective styles of discipline. When caregivers are too permissive, children do not learn to follow rules. When caregivers are overly restrictive, children may follow the rules, but as soon as they escape the oppressive regime they are likely to go wild and act out aggressively and disobediently. What is more, if children are constantly repressed, restricted, and fearful, they are unlikely to learn anything intellectual at the daycare setting.

In brief, children are more likely to learn social and intellectual skills when caregivers are stimulating and educational, responsive and respectful, moderately affectionate and appropriately demanding.[1] In our Chicago study, for instance, the children who did best had caregivers who were responsive, positive, accepting, and informative, who read to the children, offered them choices, and gave them gentle suggestions rather than simply hugging, holding, or helping them and rather than directing, controlling, or punishing them. These kinds of behavior were associated with poorer development: caregivers who initiated more physical contact, physical help, and physical control had children who did more poorly in the assessments we made of their social and mental competence. In the Child Care Staffing study as well, the children who did best had caregivers who were more sensitive, responsive, and emotionally involved, and less harsh in their discipline. These children were more involved and purposeful in the daycare setting and performed better on tests of verbal abilities outside the classroom.[2]

Training and experience. What is it, then, that makes some caregivers more positive and effective than others? Can you be sure of what kind of care your child will be getting if you know the daycare provider's background?

Does it make a difference how much training or education or experience the caregiver has? The answer to this last question is a qualified yes. Studies show that caregivers who are most likely to behave in these positive ways are those with more training and experience as childcare professionals—at least up to a certain point.[3]

Most teachers are surprisingly ignorant about child development. In one study, 53 teachers from 20 daycare centers in Delaware were given a test to assess their knowledge of child development.[4] Most of them did quite poorly; on the average, these teachers got only slightly more than half the questions correct. With more training in child development, daycare providers are more knowledgeable, and they are also more interactive, helpful, talkative, playful, positive, and affectionate with the children in their care. What is more, the children in their care are more involved, cooperative, persistent, and learn more.[5]

This association between training and quality of care has appeared in so many studies that caregiver training is now generally considered to be a sine qua non of high-quality care. But one should not conclude from this that caregiver training is a guarantee of good care or that a caregiver with a higher level of training will necessarily provide better care than one with less. Although having no training in child development is clearly worse than having some, taking ten courses is not necessarily better than taking five. It depends on the content and quality and variety of the courses. As it is, with the training currently taken by childcare workers in America, there is some evidence that when teachers have taken *more* training in child development, they develop an academic orientation, which translates in the daycare classroom into an emphasis on school activities (reading, counting, lessons, learning) to the exclusion of activities to promote a child's social or emotional development. Formal training in child development may indeed be good background for providing a daycare environment that promotes children's intellectual learning, but it is not necessarily so good for children in other ways. In our study in Chicago, the caregivers who had had more formal training in child development had children who were advanced intellectually but were significantly less competent in interactions with their peers. Caregivers who had a moderate level of training had children who did well in both social and cognitive realms.

The caregiver's general education may also predict more positive behavior in the daycare setting, although this link has not been found as consistently. In the Child Care Staffing study, though, daycare teachers with college degrees were significantly more sensitive and appropriate in their care, less harsh and emotionally detached than teachers who did not have college degrees.[6] Teachers who had a bachelor's degree in early childhood education, in particular, did more appropriate caregiving, were more sensitive and less detached, than teachers with training at a vocational institution or high school.

Another factor that predicts caregivers' behavior is their previous experience. With fewer than two or three years of experience in childcare, there is a tendency for daycare providers to simply go along with children and not initiate any educational activities. With more professional childcare experience, caregivers are likely to be more stimulating, responsive, accepting, and positive[7]— but only up to a certain point. With more than ten years of experience, there is a tendency for teachers and caregivers to be less stimulating, stricter, and more controlling.[8] Thus caregivers' experience is not a guarantee of good care, but a moderate amount of experience clearly helps.

Does the sex of the caregiver make a difference? Do women provide the best care for young children? The sex of the caregiver does seem to make a definite difference in teaching styles and behaviors. Although both men and women teachers are likely to encourage what might be considered more feminine behavior (sitting quietly, reading, painting, working on puzzles) in both boys and girls in daycare, male teachers are less likely to do this and, for boys at least, this has an advantage for their academic achievement.[9] It is unfortunate that, in the United States at least, men have been discouraged from entering the childcare field. Children can benefit from interactions with both men and women in daycare.

Stability and consistency. Another factor that influences the quality of care caregivers offer is the length of time they have been in the particular daycare setting. Child-development experts have decried the rapid turnover of personnel in daycare centers, the alacrity with which home care providers go out of business, and the tendency of babysitters to move on. They have been less vocal about "peer turnover" and the tendency of families themselves to change the child's care arrangement, but this also occurs with great frequency, and possibly with similar results. Studies that have followed children over a period of time have found that approximately half of them have changed to a new care arrangement within one year, 30 percent within six months.[10] Children are particularly likely to have new care arrangements if they are over one year of age and if care had been provided by an unrelated, unlicensed sitter who was young, inexperienced, and taking care of only one or two children. They are most likely to change from a home arrangement to a center arrangement.[11]

What effect does this kind of instability have on

children's development? Two studies have shown that, as children spend more time in a daycare setting, caregivers form closer relationships with the children (and possibly with their mothers) and become more like the mother in their behavior (more affectionate, verbal, and responsive).[12] It might be expected that this would be good for the child. Terence Moore, in England, tried to find out whether stable daycare was better for children than unstable care. In his study, six-year-old children who had more than two changes of care arrangement were found to be more insecure, fearful, and clingy; they did not do as well on psychological tests as children in stable arrangements.[13] This conforms to other research showing that when children's environments are unstable, because of changes in parents' work, health, or finances, this affects children's feelings of security and anxiety.[14]

But development is not always hindered by changing care arrangements. In another study, researchers found that there was no difference in children's social competence if the children had changed daycare centers.[15] It may be that the detrimental effects observed by Moore were the result of other instabilities in the families of these children, beyond changes in their daycare arrangements. Being exposed to more than one caregiver can provide variety and enrichment, can temper the effects of extreme caregiver styles, and can teach the child to adapt to different people. Change in itself is not necessarily bad for development, and staying with a poor caregiver is undoubtedly worse for children than changing to a good one.

The length of time the caregiver stays in the daycare setting is more clearly related to negative outcomes. The more staff members who leave the center and are replaced over the course of a year, the worse for the program—and the children. In the Child Care Staffing study, centers with the highest rates of staff turnover were rated lowest on overall quality, and the children there spent the most time aimlessly wandering and did the worst on intelligence tests.[16]

But just because a high turnover rate is associated with poor care, this does not mean that the longer the caregivers stay in a center, the better the quality of care. When a caregiver stays in one facility for three or four years, this is better than staying for only a year or two. But beyond this length of time, there is no evidence that staying longer improves the quality of care.[17]

Staff stability is an important aspect of daycare quality, not only because it is good for children to form relationships with their daily caregivers and vice versa, but also because such stability indicates that the center offers good working conditions, adequate wages, and high staff morale. In the Child Care Staffing study, centers with higher turnover paid their teachers lower wages. Teachers who were paid only $4.00 an hour or less left at twice the rate of those who earned over $6.00 an hour. In fact, the most common suggestion in that study for how to improve childcare quality, made by 90 percent of the teachers interviewed, was to pay caregivers better salaries. The best predictor of staff instability was wages. Teachers who left to take better-paying jobs were replaced with caregivers who were new to the field, less sensitive, untrained, and poorly educated.

Parents

Daycare providers are neither the first nor the most important of the child's caregivers. Parents are first and continue to be foremost. Remember that even if children spend 40 hours a week in daycare, that leaves 128 hours for them to be at home with their parents. The observations and interviews that researchers have used to study parents and children suggest quite clearly that, even though the parents of children in daycare are not totally responsible for their children's development, they do continue to have a substantial influence—just as much as if the children were at home.[18]

The affection parents express, through close physical contact, nurturance, and sensitivity to their children's needs, is clearly related to the children's feelings of security and affection toward the parents. When parents are consistently angry or rejecting, children reward them with irritability, aggression, and emotional problems. When parents are affectionate and supportive, children are happy and affectionate in return.

If parents' rejection is combined with strict discipline, its effect goes beyond the children's relations with the parents and their behavior at home; it affects their whole approach to life. Rejecting parents who use heavy-handed, restrictive discipline have children who are likely to be fearful, submissive, withdrawn, and dull. Rejecting parents who are permissive in their discipline, or permissive at first and then strict later on, have children who are likely to be hostile, aggressive, and disobedient. Showing affection and love reduces the likelihood of finding these patterns of fearful withdrawal or hostile aggression. When parents are affectionate and use strict, authoritarian discipline, children are most likely to become dependent, polite, obedient, conforming, and compliant. When parents are affectionate and permissive in discipline, children are likely to be active, outgoing, and creative, but perhaps immature. The optimal pattern of discipline for encouraging children's independence and sociability, though, is a balance between these extremes, combining warmth and affection, nurturance and sensitivity, with a moderate amount of control. Parents who use this kind of discipline set firm limits for the child, but the limits are reasonable and not too numerous. Their demands are consistent and given with rational explanations. Both social responsibility and independent autonomy are encouraged in the child. Children whose parents act in this way have been observed to be friendly, cooperative, self-reliant, independent, and happy—not only at home but in daycare as well.

Parents also foster their children's intellectual development by teaching and playing with them. As early as six months, infants whose mothers rock, jiggle, talk to, and play with them are more advanced in their development than infants whose mothers are less involved, and this relation continues as children get older. The more the parents provide appropriate materials and arrange intellectual experiences, share, expand, and elaborate the child's activities, focus the child's attention on exploring objects, entertain and talk to the child—in brief, the more stimulating the quality of their behavior—the more children learn. Especially important is simply talking to children. The more parents talk to their children, the better it is for a child's intellectual development. But parents who talk a lot to their children will also modify their speech so that it is at an appropriate level of understanding. They use shorter, simpler, and more repetitive sentences than they would with an adult. They accept the child's often painfully inadequate first efforts to speak, not intolerantly criticizing inadequacies. They talk about objects and activities that the child is looking at or playing with.

Responding to the child's needs and interests is particularly important for encouraging development. From the beginning, interaction with the infant should not be at the parent's whim, but should mesh with the infant's needs and schedule. Later, in the preschool years, responding to the child's interests, demands, questions, and expectations in ways that are appropriate and stimulating is one strategy for encouraging children to continue to ask questions and to explore. Parents can also increase the likelihood that children will behave in particularly desirable ways (whether sitting quietly or feeding the puppy) by responding to these actions in positive ways—giving praise or rewards—when they occur.

In sum, parents serve many of the same roles as day-care providers, including those of teacher, disciplinarian, provider of materials, sensitive responder, and choreographer of experiences. In addition, parents provide a foundation of stability and warmth.

Working mothers. The many demands of full-time employment make fulfilling these multiple roles of parenthood a particular challenge for working mothers. Although researchers have discovered that working mothers spend just about the same amount of time in child-related activities as nonworking mothers do, what is the quality of the time that working mothers are able to spend with their children? Do working mothers try harder—attempting to compensate for leaving their children by offering them special times and treats—or does exhaustion at the end of the day dull the quality of working mothers' interactions with their children?

In one study, observations of family interactions made at home at the end of the workday showed working mothers playing and talking with their children more than nonworking mothers.[19] This observation suggested that working mothers may indeed set aside special times to be with their children. But not all studies have revealed this difference.[20] We do not know how common these special times are or how often working mothers' interactions have this stimulating quality.

In a "standard" situation, when researchers have asked mothers to come to a room at the university and play with their children, dress them, and read to them, or when researchers have asked mothers questions about their behavior with their children at home, no differences have been found between working and nonworking mothers.[21] What seems likely is that the end of the day is an especially social time for working mothers and their children and not for mothers who are home all day, but that at other times the quality of interactions with children is similar.

More important in predicting the quality of the mother's behavior than simply whether she is employed is how happy she is in what she does. The mother's satisfaction with being a worker or a homemaker is a better predictor of how she will act with her child than simply whether she is employed. Women who are satisfied are consistently more warm, involved, playful, stimulating, and effective with their children than those who are not.[22] In one study by Ellen Hock, whether the mother was working full time or part time or not at all was not related to how well her baby did on tests or how close and secure the relationship between them was; but if a mother who was not working thought it was better to be working, or if a working mother thought she should be the baby's exclusive caregiver, the child's relations with the mother were disturbed.[23] The children of these dissatisfied and conflicted mothers were likely to respond to the mother's approaches with avoidance or crying. In another study, it was also found that infants of mothers who were homemakers and preferred it that way were more sociable than those of discontented homemakers who wished they were working.[24] With older children too, it has been found that the child's self-esteem and adjustment are better when the mother is satisfied with her role as worker or housewife.[25]

In one of the most carefully controlled studies on this subject, researcher Anita Farel interviewed 212 mothers of kindergarten children from eight schools, half of them working mothers and half nonworking. She also tested their children's persistence, creativity, curiosity, intelligence, consideration, and sociability.[26] As expected, children whose mothers were not working but who thought it would be better if they were did more poorly on almost all of these tests. Surprisingly, though, children whose mothers were working but thought they should not be working (another dissatisfied group) did not do more poorly on the tests.

Why did these children not show the expected problems? Perhaps the reason was that the children were not exposed to as much of their mother's dissatisfaction, since she was away from them more, at work. Perhaps it was because these children had special times with their mothers that compensated for her dissatisfaction. Perhaps it was because they were in daycare arrangements that provided the stimulation and care the mother could not. Perhaps it was because the message conveyed by unhappy working mothers was basically accepting of the child—these mothers wanted to be with their children more—whereas the message of the discontented full-time mothers was more rejecting: by working, they would have more time away from the child. Or perhaps mothers wanted to spend less time with children who were not developing too well. Whatever the reason, it is clear that the mother's work status alone did not determine the children's development. How the mother felt about herself and her roles as worker and mother, not simply the fact that she worked, was what predicted children's development and well-being.

The Differences

Daycare providers compensate for the time that parents are not available. Daycare providers teach and discipline, respond with food and hugs, just as parents do. Caregivers in daycare and at home may both contribute to the child's learning and development. But a daycare provider is not the same as a mother; a daycare teacher is not just like dad. Caregivers are unlikely to be as invested in the children as parents are, and they do not have the same power to make important decisions. They usually have more training; they often have more experience taking care of children. But just how differently do they act?

A number of researchers have investigated this question. In one study, by Robert Hess and his colleagues, 67 mothers of children attending daycare centers and 34 of their teachers were interviewed and observed interacting with the child in specified tasks.[27] When the adults were asked about their goals and expectations for young children, mothers and teachers agreed on many things: in valuing independence and social skills over academic abilities, for example. But teachers thought that children's independence, emotional maturity, and expressiveness were more important than mothers did, and mothers thought politeness, social graces, and school skills more important than teachers did. These values went along with the disciplinary and management strategies each favored. Teachers appealed to rational rules and explanations; they were more flexible and permissive than mothers. Their requests were indirect and moderated: "Please put this block where it belongs." "I wonder how these blocks are alike. I wish you would tell me." "Can you tell me why you put that one there?" They preferred to let children initiate actions rather than telling them how to do the task. Mothers, by contrast, were more direct, demanding, and task-oriented; they appealed to their own authority rather than abstract rules and made explicit corrections when the child made a mistake: "Put that block there." "Tell me why you put that block there." "No, put the other block there."

The results of this study are consistent with those of other studies. In a daycare center, teachers are more permissive, more tolerant of disobedience and aggression, and less inclined to set standards for children's behavior than mothers are at home. They justify their requests, explain their reasons, and help children find solutions. They join in play with the children and emphasize learning through play. Mothers tend to find these care providers not strict enough, not sufficiently school-teacherish. They themselves are more authoritarian and demanding with their children. They talk more often and have more extended and far-ranging conversations at home than teachers do in the center. Their talk is likely to be social chatting, talk about do's and don't's, about past and future events, about what's happening at the moment. Children are more nearly equal participants in these conversations at home; they ask more questions and give more answers.[28]

The different conversational styles of mothers and teachers are illustrated in the excerpts below, taken from transcripts made during observations of one four-year-old, Ann, playing at home and in nursery school.[29]

At home

Ann: Come look at their little bit of hair.

Mother: Love, I'm just looking for Ben's shorts. I don't know what he has done with them.

Ann: Hum, look at his . . . Mum look at his little sch . . . look at his little h . . . Mummy, he's got a little bit hair, so come and have a look.

Mother: Blue hair (laughs).

Ann: What's wrong with blue hair?

Mother: Well, I don't know, it can be fair hair, or brown hair, or red hair.

Ann: Don't have red hair (indignant).

Mother: Some people do. Know that boy in the park yesterday?

Ann: Yeah.

Mother: With a kite.

Ann: Yeah, Mummy.

Mother: He had what you call red hair, auburn. You know Daddy?

Ann: Mm.

Mother: He used to have red hair before it went grey.

At nursery school

Teacher: What are you going to call your babies?

Teacher: Hm?

Teacher: What are you going to call your twins? Ann?

Ann: Emily and Katy.

Teacher: Emily . . .?

Ann: And Katy.

Teacher: Katy! Supposing they're boys? You can't call twins that if they're boys, can you? (laughs). (Ann laughs and goes off.)

Home daycare providers present another pattern of behavior in their interactions with children, one that is different from both nursery-school or daycare-center teachers and mothers. Compared to teachers, home care providers interact more with each child individually, especially when there are only one or two children in the care arrangement, and they may be more positive and sensitive in their approach to children. They also do more supervisory disciplining. Compared to mothers, daycare home providers are cooler and more emotionally aloof, less playful and stimulating. They don't kiss or caress the children as often and are less tuned in to their individual interests.[30]

Although these generalizations are based on averages, which hide the enormous diversity found within each category of caregiver, they do suggest that in the child's life different kinds of caregivers are likely to exhibit different styles of behavior. Mothers are likely to be loving and involved, salient and important, directive and effective; they give the child security, confidence, trust, and affection, exhibit strong emotions of love, joy, pain, and anger; they give basic socialization training (such as when and where to go to the toilet) and teach social rules and graces, moral norms and lessons, and conversational skills. Home daycare providers offer discipline and socialization without the emotional investment the parents feel and, building on the trust and confidence the child develops at home, provide the child with some variety and relief from the intensity of family interaction. Teachers in daycare centers and nursery schools foster the children's independence, self-sufficiency, and self-direction, providing formal education, intellectual knowledge, and opportunities for positive interaction with other children that increase the child's social competence. Children in daycare can benefit from exposure to *all* these different styles. As long as the family provides a secure foundation, exposure to other caregivers is an enriching part of these children's early experience.

8/ Infants and Individuals

Each child is a unique individual, and there are limits to how much we can use research on daycare to make decisions for any one child. Research is based on statistical probabilities, not absolute truths. Research applies to groups of children, not individuals. If a significant difference is found between daycare and home-care children, in one study or several, this means that children in daycare are more likely than children at home to behave this way. It does not mean that every child in daycare will behave that way. Just as the weatherman can predict only a 60 percent chance of rain on a particular day, so research can only predict that, other things equal, there is a greater probability that a child will behave in a certain way if he or she is in daycare. Just as, even after hearing the weather forecast, each person has to decide whether to take an umbrella, each parent must determine whether to put a particular child in daycare. Research only gives the odds, no guarantees.

Because research is based on averages and ignores differences among children, I have not talked about individual children in this book. Here I get a little closer to talking about individuals by discussing variations in daycare effects for different kinds of children. But, still, even this discussion is about averages. It may be helpful to know how effects differ for these different groups of children—boys and girls, infants and preschoolers, easy and difficult children, healthy and ill ones—but this will not tell you how *your* child is going to do. The purpose of the discussion is to underline the need to interpret everything researchers have to say about daycare in terms of your individual situation, your unique child.

Boys and Girls

Researchers have documented scientifically what everyone has known all along, that boys and girls behave differently.[1] Even as young as two or three years of age, boys and girls act in ways that foreshadow their adult roles. Boys are more aggressive and competitive (especially with other boys), more physically energetic and assertive, and, given a choice of toys, go for bicycles, crates, cars, and guns, and play soccer and bad guys. Girls are more quiet and compliant, cooperative, friendly and compassionate, socially skilled and socially aware; they select dolls, dressups, and domestic toys, and play house. These differences show up all across the world. They persist even in the face of parents' conscious efforts to raise more socially responsible sons and self-assertive daughters. They are patterns that children themselves are aware of by the time they are two years old.

What happens when boys and girls go into daycare? In daycare homes, caregivers act much the same as mothers do, in ways that permit or support these stereotypical patterns,[2] so no major change would be expected and none is found. But some people have suggested that attendance in a daycare center or nursery school should reduce the stereotyped differences between boys and girls. They have predicted that boys attending daycare would be more cooperative and socially aware than boys who do not have this experience, that girls would be more independent and assertive. This seems a reasonable expectation, since boys in daycare programs have many opportunities to be sociable and girls have many opportunities to be independent.

Based on the available research, however, what seems to happen is that although boys in daycare do indeed become more sociable than boys at home, and although girls in daycare do increase in autonomy, problem solving, and even belligerence, this does not wipe out the differences between the sexes. Why not? It turns out that boys in daycare gain in independence and belligerence even as they are becoming more sociable, and girls in daycare gain in social skills even as they are becoming more independent. So boys in daycare are still more independent and loud and aggressive than girls in daycare, and girls in daycare are still more socially skilled and quiet than boys in daycare. Although teachers encourage both boys and girls to do quiet, academic tasks and discourage both boys and girls from aggression, they (and the other children) still tend to criticize girls for playing with boys and engaging in boyish activities and criticize boys for doing girlish things.[3] The gender-stereotyped differences remain in daycare just as at home. It is hard to get away from the gender roles that permeate our society, and daycare does not make boys ladylike or girls macho.

Are there other differences in the effects of daycare on boys and girls? Differences in intellectual development or emotional well-being, for example? It has frequently been documented that boys are more vulnerable to events in the environment, girls more resilient. From the time of conception to old age, females are less likely to have problems, more likely to survive. Is this difference between males and females reflected in different effects of daycare on boys and girls? Are boys worse off, girls, better off, in daycare? The answer is a weak maybe. There is *limited* evidence that there is a slight disadvantage for boys to be in daycare and a slight advantage for girls.

First, in some studies, boys placed in daycare in infancy were found to develop less secure relationships with their mothers, whereas the relationships girls formed with their mothers were not affected by being in daycare.[4] Second, boys in daycare are more likely to develop undesirable behavior, such as disobedience and aggression; girls do not have a problem with aggression because they tend to be less aggressive than boys in the first place. A girl's increased independence as a result of being in daycare is more likely to be considered a positive outcome by employed mothers, who are themselves independent females. Third, some studies have indicated that girls are more likely to benefit from the academic advantages of participating in educational programs than boys are. In one study of more than 2,000 one- to four-year-old children, the offspring of a nationally representative sample of women in their twenties, girls who were in daycare, particularly in centers, were intellectually advanced over girls who were at home (an average of fifteen points on one IQ test); boys from high-income families who were in full-time daycare in the first year of life had somewhat slower intellectual development than boys from high-income families who were at home.[5]

But before you decide to put your daughter in daycare or stay home with your son, consider this. These findings do not appear in every study. An analysis of the effects of daycare for a combined sample from more than twelve different studies did not reveal significant differences overall for boys and girls in the quality of the relationships they formed with their mothers.[6] If there is a dif-

ference in the effect of daycare on emotional development for boys and girls, therefore, it is quite small. If
there is a difference in the effect of daycare on intellectual
development, this difference too is not inevitable. In our
study in Chicago, it was boys more than girls who appeared to benefit from being in structured daycare programs.

What parents should take from the results of research
on daycare effects for boys and girls, then, is not that
boys are necessarily going to have more problems if they
are in daycare but that, because boys in general are more
susceptible to environmental conditions, we should be
especially careful about the kind and quality of daycare
for boys. Boys might do best in daycare with a structured
curriculum, in a setting where particular attention is paid
to teaching children how to get along with each other,
and in a daily arrangement that allows the boy ample
time to be with his mother.

The research on the effects of daycare on boys and girls
raises a theme that appears repeatedly in the research
comparing the effects of daycare for different groups of
children: children who are more vulnerable in general
are more likely to be affected by daycare.

Children of Different Ages

Another group of children who are especially vulnerable
is infants. Would it be better for mothers to wait until
children are two or three or four years old before going
back to work? Are infants affected by their experiences
in daycare more than older children are? Does it matter
at what age children begin daycare?

Infants. There are many reasons to expect that daycare
would have a profound effect on infants. Babies are fresh

and new and untouched; whatever happens to them is more likely to make an impression. Babies are at the beginning of their lives; what happens early in life can affect what happens later. They require special attention and sensitivity from their caregivers. *All* their needs must be met by each caregiver—needs for food and safety and attention and care, not just for play or education. Babies need protection, love, nurturance, and responsiveness, as well as stimulation. They are dependent on the caregiver to watch, to listen, to act. They need interesting things to look at and hold, safe things to chew and explore. They need not to be left in the crib or playpen alone to sleep all day. Babies can't express themselves in words to tell the caregiver what's wrong; they can't move around to get the attention they need. They need a caregiver who can read their signals and expressions and is concerned enough to do so. Basically, infants need adults; they do not need to be with other children.

In the last few years, there has been a heated debate about whether infants should be in daycare at all: does it make them emotionally insecure and socially maladjusted? The major source of the debate is research on infants' developing relations with their mothers. The infant-mother relationship is, of course, central in every individual's psychological development. Over the course of the first year of life, every infant must develop a strong emotional feeling for the person who cares for him, plays with him, and loves him. This feeling of attachment distinguishes the primary caregiver from other more casual companions. The child wants to be near this person, especially in times of stress, fatigue, or illness, to hold and be held by her, to keep her in view or at least at his beck and call. He prefers her company and contact to anyone else's. If they must be separated, he is distressed when she leaves. This fond feeling becomes obvious by the end of the first year and continues to be evident over the next several years. Most often, the first object of the child's affection is the mother. If a father or an older sibling is centrally involved in the child's life, the child soon develops attachments to these people too.

But when the infant is separated from these people for eight or ten or more hours a day, the relationships are at risk. Research has shown, however, that infants whose mothers work full time do form strong attachments to them.[7] Infants may also form affectionate relationships with their daycare providers and prefer these caregivers to strangers. But daycare children still overwhelmingly prefer their mothers. They go to their mother for help, stay close to her, approach her more often, interact with her more, and rely on her rather than the caregiver when distressed or bored.[8] In the daycare center, they do not greet the teacher in the morning with the same joy heaped on the mother at night. They do not behave as if the caregiver is a substitute mother—nor is this how caregivers perceive themselves.

But the question is whether the quality of the relationships daycare children have with their mothers is as good, as emotionally secure, as the relationships of infants who are being raised exclusively at home. As a first step in answering this question, we can look at data from all studies of infants in daycare that have included the same method of measuring children's attachments. Almost twenty studies have used a single standard to study the mother-child relationship. Putting together the results reveals that the infants who are in daycare full time, compared with infants who are in daycare part time or not at all, are more likely to be classified as having insecure relationships with their mothers.[9]

The problem is how to interpret this finding. Does the standard assessment used really reflect emotional insecurity in these children? If it does, is the difference large enough to require concern? To appreciate the problem, we must first consider the standard method of measuring the children's relationships with their mothers, the so-called Strange Situation. The scenario goes like this: An infant, his mother nearby, plays with toys in an unfamiliar room; he is left by the mother alone in the room with an unfamiliar woman; he plays with the stranger in the mother's absence; the stranger leaves; the mother returns and picks him up. Some children in this situation cling to their mothers and won't even let them leave the room. Other children ignore the mother's departure. They continue playing with toys or the stranger, and when the mother returns they actively avoid her. Still other children are ambivalent in their reactions— clinging to the mother one minute and spurning her the next. Most children show a balanced pattern that has been called a "secure" attachment. They are able to leave the mother's side to explore the toys and the room, but they clearly prefer to be with her rather than the stranger, and as the mother begins her comings and goings at the researcher's request, they show more and more concern and are more likely to stay close to her. They always greet her enthusiastically when she returns to the room. The child's attachment is measured by observing how he responds at the final step of the scenario, when the mother returns to the room to pick him up. If the child goes to or greets the mother, this is a sign of a secure relationship. If the child avoids or ignores her, this is a sign that the relationship is not secure.

Unfortunately, though, there are problems in using this method with daycare infants, because the scenario sounds suspiciously like the kind of experience infants in daycare have all the time. Could it be that infants who have had this kind of experience more often are less likely to seek physical closeness with their mothers? When other methods of measuring infants' relationships with their mothers are used, it turns out, the differences are not as marked.

We must also question whether, even if babies do have less balanced relationships with their mothers, it means they are emotionally insecure. On other measures of emotional adjustment, children who were in daycare when they were infants have been observed to do as well as children who were not—suggesting that daycare infants are not more insecure in general.

Also, even if the observed difference in these infants' relationships with their mothers does indicate a degree of emotional insecurity, is the difference large enough to cause concern? Among the more than 1,200 children in these studies, 64 percent of those who were in daycare full time were classified as securely attached to their mothers, compared to 71 percent of the children who were not in daycare. Is this rate of 64 percent too low? It turns out to be within the normal range. Combining data from many studies in cultures around the world, the overall rate of secure attachment to the mother is 65 percent.[10] The significance of the observed difference in our culture, therefore, lies not in demonstrating that daycare is harmful to infants but in alerting us to possible problems that daycare *may* create for infants.

The results of these studies suggest that we need to be cautious as we try out different forms and programs of daycare for infants. We should be cautious about the number of hours infants are in care; infants in care for only twenty hours per week were not more likely to exhibit insecure attachment in the Strange Situation. We should be careful about the quality of daycare. In daycare centers offering poor-quality care, infants' cognitive learning as well as their emotional development are likely to be affected detrimentally.[11] We know much less about daycare quality for infants than we do about daycare for older children; daycare for preschoolers has been around much longer and is much more common. We need to study carefully the kinds of training and personal qualities that make care providers good caregivers for infants. We need to keep a close eye on the number of infants the caregiver is responsible for. It is clear that no caregiver, regardless of training, can provide adequate care and stimulation for seven or eight infants, let alone evacuate them in an emergency. Yet there are states that allow this kind of care.

The sad fact is that, right now, the quality of care for these most vulnerable children, the youngest participants in daycare, includes the worst available. State regulations covering daycare for infants and toddlers range from excellent to abysmal.[12] Only three states require that daycare facilities have one caregiver for every three infants; only 27 states require one caregiver for every four infants. Because of the expense of caregivers' salaries, having an adult-child ratio of one to three is economically unfeasible without financial support from the government or other sources. In the current climate, then, it is the rare daycare center that can provide the kind of care that infants need. In fact, it is the rare center that takes infants at all. Home daycare is an alternative, but unless grandmother is available, this option also requires careful screening to find a caregiver who will offer high-quality care.

Toddlers. Toddlers are a little hardier than infants. They can make their wishes known more clearly, as they talk and say no. They are more likely to understand the caregiver's requests and are beginning to understand a conversation. But toddlers still need much attention from care providers. They are still emotionally dependent on adult support, love, approval, interaction, and interpretation. They need adults to give them courage, to give meaning to their experiences, and to help them learn about the world—to explain about fire engines and trains, birds and planes, to make sense of their jumbled impressions. Toddlers need caregivers who describe and explain and answer their questions. It is essential for children of this age, like younger infants, to be in daycare with an adequate number of adults to care for them. Research on children of this age shows that they are particularly affected by being in large classes with few caregivers.[13]

Toddlers are also susceptible to strict discipline. The "terrible twos" get their reputation from their overuse of the word *no*. The challenge for caregivers is to accept the toddlers' *no* as part of growing up and expressing themselves, and to convince the children of what to do rather than making them do it. Toddlers need gentle and skillful management, not a show of force.

In the toddler stage, children also begin to like being with other children. But they are not very good at sharing, and in fact they are generally not as interested in the other children as in the toys they play with. It is especially important that daycare for toddlers have lots of materials and lots of space for exploring.

Toddlers are also beginning to understand that mother will be back later. They understand, but still, if they start daycare at this age, they are likely to protest. Few of us like leaving the nest, at any age. Despite their protests, children placed in daycare at two years of age have been found to adapt to daycare better than those who start later, acting less withdrawn, dependent, defiant, or hostile.[14] In terms of cognitive learning or achievement of social competence, however, the age of starting daycare does not seem to matter. Children often exhibit gains in learning after six to twelve months in daycare, whether they are two or three or four years old when they begin.[15]

Preschoolers. Within the preschool period, there is some evidence that children who start before age four do better than those who start later.[16] They have a longer time to learn the lessons the program offers, to adapt to being in a group, to develop relationships with other children and the caregivers. Preschoolers are much more ready than infants or toddlers to take on the world. They are developing independent interests and can communicate more easily. They are ready for a social life with peers. But although they enjoy doing things with other children, their friendships are fleeting. So are their attention spans. They like playing pretend, building, painting, and sometimes counting and reciting letters; they like hearing stories and watching TV. But they have trouble paying attention—to lessons or play—for very long. Care providers often overestimate what preschoolers can do and for how long. Preschoolers can't plan ahead; they want to rush into things. They still need adults to guide their activities. They need intimacy and comfort from caregivers, patient explanations and answers to their endless questions, and gentle management of their unruly impulses. They need to be encouraged to work on projects that call for effort and involvement over time, projects that are not academic but deal with things they are interested in. Their activities should not be all work or all play, but meaningful involvement in both. In the preschool years, it is probably more important to focus on the quality of the caregiver's behavior than on the number of children or adults in the setting.

Easy and Difficult Children

"Difficult" infants cry intensely and often, spit out or refuse new foods, sleep irregularly and briefly, and adapt to change and new situations slowly; "easy" infants do not—and this difference in temperament persists throughout childhood. Several researchers have studied how adjustment to daycare is related to individual temperaments. Craig Ramey and his colleagues followed infants from the time they were placed in the Frank Porter Graham daycare center until they were three years old.[17] In the first year of life, easy infants did better (in terms of cognitive development) than difficult ones, whether they were at home or in the center. But easy infants did even better in the center than they did at home, whereas difficult ones did worse. After a year in this model daycare center, there was no longer a difference in the effect of daycare on children of different temperaments; both easy and difficult children were learning more in the center. What temperament seems to do is make the initial adjustment to daycare (a new and complex situation) harder: difficult children do better with a familiar, simpler caregiving situation, where they have more individualized care.

This need does not go away if the children start daycare when they are older. Researchers have studied older children entering nursery school.[18] Again, the initial adjustment was more problematic for children who had been identified as difficult or "slow to warm up" in infancy. But later the progress made by these children depended on the type of program they were in. In highly structured, formal, somewhat restrictive programs, easy children adapted readily; difficult children adapted eventually; slow-to-warm-up children withdrew; extremely active or hyperactive children acted out. In open programs, easy children adapted readily; slow-to-warm-up children adapted slowly; active children remained active but were not necessarily negative; and difficult children went on being difficult, giving frequent and irritating responses. Easy children thrive in any program—they are involved and happy, follow the rules, and get along with teachers and the other children. Other kinds of children need special care and consideration in the choice of a daycare program. Once again, we need to pay particular attention to the daycare arrangements made for more vulnerable children—in this case, more vulnerable because of their temperaments.

Sick and Well Children

This theme is echoed when children have health problems. Data from the National Longitudinal Study of Youth, for instance, suggest that daycare provides significant intellectual input that can enhance children's IQ only if the children are healthy. For children with health problems, it does not offer this advantage. In fact, for infant boys with health problems, social-emotional and motor development were most helped by being cared for more extensively by their mothers.[19]

Trouble at Home

Some children are vulnerable because they are born with more difficult temperaments or physical problems; others may have difficulties because they are born into families with problems. There may be money problems, poor health, or mental illness in the family. Unfortunately, children from difficult home situations do not improve their condition simply by going into daycare. Although it is true that children from low-income families gain from good daycare in terms of their physical and academic development,[20] children from families with problems are still at a relative disadvantage, even in daycare. Children from families with fewer problems gain more from their daycare experience than do children from families with more problems.[21] Children from homes disturbed by divorce, violence, neglect, or illness, children whose parents are inaccessible and insensitive, children who are unable to form close and secure relationships with their parents, are withdrawn and anxious in daycare. They are unwilling to leave their mothers to play with other children, less helpful and friendly with these other children, less likely to interact positively with the caregiver, less likely to comply with adult rules in the daycare setting. They have more difficulty adjusting to daycare.[22] Children from families with problems have difficulties wherever they go, and daycare is no solution.

The difficulties, however, can be aggravated by daycare in which the caregiver has little insight or warmth. It might be thought that children from families with problems would do better in daycare homes than centers, since they could get more individual attention from the caregiver and there would be less stress and strangeness. But this seems unlikely unless the daycare provider is particularly supportive and sensitive. It could be argued just as plausibly that children from problem homes might do better in a busy, playful, cheerful daycare center, which is more clearly different from the home environment where the problems exist. It is impossible to say that one type of daycare or another would be most suitable for these children. What is important is that they are given special attention and consideration wherever they are, and that they are placed in a particularly good daycare setting, whatever type it is.

Finding the daycare setting that is best for any individual child is the inevitable challenge that faces each parent. In the next chapter I give some guidelines for recognizing daycare of high quality, daycare that will be most likely to foster the learning and development of all children.

9/ Finding Good Care

Parents decide on a daycare arrangement by balancing three things: cost, convenience, and quality. At all income levels, the majority of parents prefer daycare in their own home, by a regular, nonrelated adult babysitter.[1] This arrangement is clearly most convenient, and with an in-home care provider parents expect that they will be able to continue their control over the child's experiences and that the caregiver will respect their views and give the child the kind of discipline they agree with.[2] But this is usually the most costly kind of daycare. For that reason many parents choose to put their children in daycare homes. Daycare homes may also be convenient, if close by, and they are flexible, familiar, and comfortable. Parents can still exert some control over their child's experiences, and this is the least expensive of all types of care.[3] If the parents' goals for the child are supervision, stimulating play, and school preparation, however, they are most likely to choose the third alternative, a daycare center or nursery school.[4] They give up some convenience to achieve these goals—especially if the center is only open half days—but since costs run from relatively inexpensive to relatively costly, they can often find a center program to fit their budget, especially if they are willing to be put on a waiting list until space is available.

It should be noted, though, that in the Child Care Settings study it was found that among programs that charge fees, those that offer higher quality also charge more.

Once they have decided what kind of daycare they want, parents usually look only for settings of that type. They start by asking neighbors, friends, sisters with children. In one study of 611 households in Detroit, 90 percent of the women using regular daycare by a nonrelative had located the daycare setting through a friend or a relative.[5] Long-time friends were found to be the most helpful for recommending daycare providers. A few women used more formal or public means of searching—newspapers, telephone directories, bulletin boards, local childcare coordinating councils—after or instead of these informal sources. But they claimed that these methods had not been very effective. If friends failed, they found that local newsletters were better for finding babysitters, city social-service departments were better for finding daycare homes, and just driving around was the best way to find centers. Only 15 percent of the women surveyed said it had been a problem to find daycare, but half of them claimed that they would have used an information-referral system if one had been available. Such systems, once a rarity, are now becoming more common.

After a decision about the desired type of care has been made and one facility has been located, parents usually stop searching. Most parents do not shop around; they are just glad to have found a place or person that will provide care for their child. Children are often enrolled in centers or homes, site unseen. A visit or phone call is all the checking up that many parents do. As a result, they are buying the proverbial pig in a poke. The friends who have recommended the caregiver or center have not usually known more than a few caregivers or visited more than one center. A "professional" (doctor, professor) who might have made a recommendation has not usually visited any centers. Telephone directories do not screen listed daycare facilities for quality, and newspaper ads are clearly biased. The fact that a center or a home is licensed indicates only that it meets certain minimal physical standards, not that it offers good care. Community agencies or referral services are not allowed to give parents recommendations or evaluations about quality, even if they have them. A phone call to the daycare center or babysitter is not very informative about quality unless the caller asks very astute questions and gets very accurate answers.

Even if parents visit the daycare facility, they often do not know what to look for. Suggestions given in women's magazines about how to identify a good center are usually vague, untested, and hard to interpret and observe (how can parents know what "optimal amounts of touching, holding, smiling, and looking" are, or what "balances interaction with leaving infant alone" means?). For all these reasons, most parents choose a particular daycare setting for the child on the basis of its physical condition (looks clean and smells good) and their quick rapport with the daycare director or provider.[6] It is no surprise that, in surveys of how satisfied parents are with the daycare their children are receiving, close to one third are not satisfied.[7] It goes without saying that parents should do a more thorough job of checking out the place where they plan to leave their most prized possession.

If you are thinking of putting your child in daycare, plan ahead. Begin your search at least three or four months in advance. Investigate *all* options. Call around.

Ask everyone. Find out whether your community has a resource and referral service. Use it. When you locate a daycare provider, ask questions—lots of them. Ask about enrollments. Ask about the backgrounds and training of the staff. Ask about sick care and what happens in emergencies. Ask about staff turnover. Ask how many children each caregiver is responsible for. Interview the care provider on the phone. Go to visit the facility, more than once. Go unannounced. Don't be impressed by fancy buildings; observe the children closely, look for interest, involvement, listlessness, wandering, fighting. Check the daycare provider's references. Call your city or state government; ask other parents who have used the facility. Even a visit to the place can give you only a general impression of the quality of care offered, so visit several different facilities and make systematic observations and notes. Take your time. This decision deserves at least as much time as buying a new car or a new house. Your child may spend 5,000 or more critical hours here.

How can you become better informed about what high-quality care is and tell if a daycare center is providing it? In the rest of this chapter I will suggest some of the ways to identify good daycare.

Federal Requirements

The Federal Interagency Day Care Requirements (FIDCR) are the government standards established in 1980 to regulate federally supported daycare facilities. Although these standards have never been implemented by the government, and although they do not represent "ideal" daycare, they do provide a solid minimum for quality care. Parents would do well to adopt them as their own basic standards. Very briefly, the FIDCR standards require that the daycare facility have these components:

- A planned daily program of developmentally appropriate activities that promote children's intellectual, social, emotional, and physical development. (In a daycare center, this daily schedule should be written and available to parents; for daycare homes it need not be written.)
- Trained caregivers with specialized training in childcare, who have also gone through an orientation that includes health, safety, and program procedures for that particular setting.
- Adequate and nutritious meals.
- A record of immunization for each child; information and help to parents about health services in the community.
- Opportunities for parents to observe the daycare setting and discuss the child's needs before enrollment; unlimited access to the setting to observe the child and regular opportunities to meet with the caregiver(s) to discuss the child's needs after enrollment; opportunities to participate in policy making for the setting; access to evaluations or reports on the setting.
- The following class or group sizes and staff-child ratios:

	Maximum group size	Staff-child ratio
Infants	6	1:3
Toddlers	12	1:4
Preschoolers	16	1:8

In the Child Care Staffing study it was found that centers meeting these standards paid their staffs better, had better working conditions, and had teachers with higher levels of education and more training in early childhood education.[8] The teachers provided more developmentally appropriate activities for the children, were more sensitive and less harsh in their caregiving. The children spent less time wandering and scored higher on tests of their knowledge and language ability. As a first step in deciding whether a daycare setting is likely to provide good care, then, parents should find out whether the center or home meets these minimal standards.

Guidelines from Research

A second way of deciding whether a daycare setting is likely to provide high-quality care is to use the results of research. Here are some guidelines drawn from the research discussed in this book:

- In general, center-based programs are more likely than home-based care to provide educational opportunities for children and to increase their social competence, maturity, and intellectual development.
- In general, home-based care is more likely than center-based to offer children frequent one-to-one interaction with the caregiver and discipline and training close to what the mother herself would provide.
- Daycare centers that receive some public funds are most likely to offer care of high quality. For-profit centers, especially chains, are likely to have higher staff turnover and worse staff-child ratios.
- Programs that offer children a free choice of

activities punctuated by occasional educational lessons are most likely to lead to gains in children's achievement, learning, and constructive play.

- Programs that are unstructured and permit children to play freely in a rich and varied environment are most likely to foster children's sociability, cooperation, and self-motivated exploration.
- Programs in which children are taught social problem-solving skills are least likely to promote aggression.
- High-quality experience is less likely in a crowded and disorganized space (with less than 25 square feet per child and no separated activity areas).
- Smaller centers (with fewer than 30 children) are likely to have better staff-child ratios than larger centers (with more than 60 children).
- Daycare in states with the least stringent childcare regulations is generally of lower quality.
- An environment that offers a wide variety of materials and accessible things to do is ideal. The following materials should be available: building and construction materials (blocks, Legos); structured materials (puzzles, books); artistic materials (paints, musical instruments); manipulative materials (sand, buttons, water, dough, clay); social materials (games, cards, checkers, pickup sticks); fantasy or make-believe materials (dolls, dressups); active play equipment (slides, swings, tricycles); soft, cuddly materials (cushions, pillows, sofas).
- A daycare setting in which the child is part of a small group of children, both boys and girls, with

an age range of about two years, offers more positive, cooperative, complex, and sustained interactions with both other children and the caregiver and has benefits for social development.

- Children do better in daycare groups or classes with a moderate number of children (more than 2, fewer than 10).
- The caregiver is the key to daycare quality. Children do best when caregivers are actively involved in talking, teaching, and playing; providing interesting materials; responding to the child's interests, advances, and questions; encouraging activities and making suggestions; making few demands and restrictions, no threats, criticisms, or punishments. Good care in a home or center is not indicated by an abundance of physical affection, unconditional praise, or strict discipline.
- Daycare providers who think of themselves as professionals, have been trained in child development, have had five to ten years of experience, and are part of a training and support network or an educationally oriented center are more likely to provide good care.
- The best kind of daycare varies according to the individual needs of the child. More vulnerable children need special care. For slow-to-warm-up children, good care would be slanted toward an unpressured, supportive atmosphere; for difficult children, toward more structure and consistency; active children need more latitude and less physical restrictiveness; withdrawn children may benefit from sensitive and nurturant caregiving in a busy, cheerful environment; insecure children may have trouble in any kind of daycare.

Observation Checklist

The third way parents can assess the quality of a daycare setting is to make systematic observations and interviews in the facility. A checklist to guide such observations has been developed by Marilyn Bradbard and Richard Endsley.[9] These researchers took a list of items from the literature and asked a panel of child-development experts which items they thought best reflected good daycare. Then they field-tested the checklist by having mothers and college students observe in daycare centers that had been independently rated by experts. The items that were found to differentiate between centers the experts had judged to be of high or low quality were put in a revised form of the checklist. These items did not include all the things about a daycare facility that might suggest its high quality; they were things that could be observed easily and reliably in a half-hour visit and that indicated important features of the quality of care. The Bradbard and Endsley checklist was designed for daycare centers, but I have modified it here to apply to daycare homes as well and to fit with the research-based guidelines listed above. There is no scale that goes along with the checklist to indicate when a center offers "high enough" quality. The way to use the checklist is to fill it out for a number of daycare facilities and use their *relative* scores as an indication of their *relative* quality.

Health and Safety. The first thing parents want to be sure of is that the daycare facility is safe. Here are some good signs:

- Adults do not smoke in the presence of children; air smells fresh.
- Floors are clean.

- Floors are carpeted or have nonskid covering.
- Children's eating area is clean and attractive.
- There are no children with soiled diapers or pants.
- At least one adult is present at all times to supervise children.
- Detergents, medicines, drugs are kept out of reach of children (on high shelf or in locked cabinet).
- Electrical outlets are covered with safety caps.
- First-aid supplies (soap, bandaids, gauze, thermometer) are available (ask).
- Toys and equipment are in good repair (no sharp edges, splinters, paint chips, electrical wires, loose parts on toys).
- Heavy pieces of furniture (cabinets, bookcases) are secure and stable, can't tip over on children.
- Staff keeps records on each child (emergency phone numbers, medical information).
- Woodworking or kitchen tools (hammers, scissors) and other sharp objects are used only with adult supervision.
- Climbing structures, slides, swings are not too high and are positioned over sand or bark, away from other play equipment.
- Caregivers are observed to wash their hands whenever food is being prepared or children are being diapered.
- There is an isolation area for sick children.

Abuse. In addition to being sure their children won't get slivers or cuts, parents want to be sure their children will be safe from physical or sexual abuse in the daycare facility. Fears about this were raised by several widely publicized cases of alleged multiple abuses in daycare centers in the 1980s. A comprehensive survey of all reported cases of sex abuse in daycare centers from 1983 to 1985 showed that there were 2,500 abuse victims in the three-year period. Although this number sounds alarmingly high, in fact the risk of sex abuse in daycare centers is actually less than in children's own homes. The rate of sexual abuse in daycare centers is 5 children out of every 10,000, whereas at home it is 9 out of 10,000. Less than half of these cases involved a professional childcare worker; the perpetrators were janitors, busdrivers, and family members. More often than not the perpetrator was a man (although only 5 percent of daycare staffs are male). Typically the victim was a girl. Unfortunately, the survey did not identify the types of daycare that are more likely to be scenes of abuse. The risk of abuse did seem to be less in facilities in which parents had ready access to the children (although even this was not fail-safe). Two thirds of the incidents occurred in bathrooms.

To guard against the possibility of physical or sexual abuse, look for the following:

- Parents are encouraged to drop in at any time.
- Doors to the bathrooms are open when children are using them.
- Neither daycare workers nor their family members have police records.
- Children do not play in the bathroom or engage in sex play, such as talking about or playing with their private parts or those of other children.
- Children do not look fearful, anxious, neglected.
- Arriving children do not protest being dropped off.
- No physical punishment is observed.
- There are no fewer than two adults in the room at one time.
- Workers do not tease children in inappropriate ways, such as calling them derogatory names,

making weak or strong threats, pointing out gender-specific behavior ("good little girls don't do that").

- There are rules about who can pick children up from the center.

Physical space. Beyond these guidelines for protecting children, the next thing parents should look for is a physical environment that will stimulate children's play and learning. Here are some things to check in the organization of the space in the home or center and the variety of materials available:

- Individual space (locker, drawer, cubicle) exists for each child to store personal belongings.
- Quiet space allows children to nap (shades or curtains can be closed, cots or mats can be set up in separate area or there are bedrooms).
- Storage space is available for children to return toys and equipment to shelves after use.
- Windows are low enough for children to see outside.
- Temperature and humidity are comfortable (approximately 68–79°F).
- A variety of pictures, posters, mobiles are in view.
- Toileting area is easy for children to get to.
- There is direct access to enclosed outdoor play area from the building.
- There is an outdoor play area with open space for sunny days.
- There is an outdoor play area under cover for rainy days.
- The outdoor play area is easy to supervise (no hidden areas where children cannot be seen).
- The outdoor play area is well drained and

covered with a soft surface (sand, bark, grass for tumbling, running, sitting) in one place and a hard surface (for riding toys) in another place.

- Indoor play area has soft surfaces (pillows, cushions, rugs, easy chairs, couches).
- Physical space is not overcrowded (too many children, too much large equipment).

Materials, equipment, and activities. The daycare facility contains the following:

- Attractive and well-written story and picture books.
- Paints, crayons, pencils, paste, clay or dough, sand, water, safe scissors, paper, buttons.
- Materials and equipment for quiet play (books, puzzles) and active play (riding toys, climbing structures).
- Enough materials and equipment so that children do not have to wait more than a few minutes to use them.
- Two or more of the following toys and equipment: riding toys, climbing equipment, pull toys, balance beam, pounding toys, stringing toys, nested boxes.
- Two or more of these toys and equipment: social games (checkers, pickup sticks), musical toys or instruments, toys or materials that teach the three R's (cards, puzzles, books).
- Building or construction materials: wood, cardboard, boxes, blocks, tinkertoys, Legos.
- In the outdoor play area there are two or more of the following: blocks, cartons or boards for building, sandbox and sand toys, slides, riding toys, seesaw, balance beam, tires.

- There are play areas indoors where no furniture or objects are off limits.
- Toys and play materials are accessible without asking (on low, open shelves, in toy chests).
- Children have opportunities to run and climb both indoors and outdoors.
- Children are given a choice of several activities (story, music, painting, puzzles) much of the time (except naps, mealtime, lessons).
- The day's schedule includes planned, structured activities as well as free play.
- Both boys and girls are given the full range of activities: dressups, housekeeping, and dolls for boys; climbing and riding toys, cars, trucks, and tools for girls.
- Both children and adults are involved in cleaning up after activities (clearing table, folding laundry, putting away paints).

Care providers. The behavior of caregivers is the key to good care. Look for the following:

- There are enough adults to provide individual attention (at least one for every six or seven children, more for children under three years).
- Caregivers explain clearly what they want in words children can understand, often kneeling or bending over to the child's eye level when speaking.
- Caregivers use encouragement, suggestion, and praise rather than orders, prohibitions, criticism, or reprimands.
- Caregivers respond to children's questions.
- Caregivers are observed to teach children

sometimes but not all the time (teaching may be informal, explaining, labeling, reading).
- Some sort of educational program is in evidence.
- Caregivers do not spend all their time with one child while other children have nothing to do.
- Caregivers talk to individual children, not just to groups of children.
- Male as well as female adults are employed by the center or available in the home.
- Caregivers have had some training in childcare and child development (ask).
- Caregivers are interested in childcare as a career (attend meetings, read books, are part of a daycare support network, have ties to other community agencies), not just a temporary job (ask).
- Caregivers are paid a decent wage (ask).
- No more than 20 percent of the teachers have been replaced in the last year (ask).
- There are other adults available for backup if necessary (ask).

Children. One way to assess the quality of the daycare program is to look at how involved the children are. Look for signs of happy, busy children.

- Children smile and laugh around the caregiver(s).
- Children are busy and involved (not wandering aimlessly or just sitting and staring blankly, waiting around).
- Each child spends some time interacting (playing, talking, working together) with other children.
- Children seem to enjoy one another (help, smile, show approval, play).

- No fighting (hitting, pinching, kicking, grabbing toys) is observed.
- Conflicts are settled with some adult intervention.
- Children are in relatively small classes or groups: in centers, 16–18 preschoolers, 11–12 toddlers, 6–7 infants; in daycare homes, 3–4 children.
- Both boys and girls are present.
- Age spread of children is about 2 years.
- Children are observed choosing a new activity on their own.
- Different children are observed doing different activities.

Parents. You are going to be part of the daycare arrangement too. How do you *feel* about the caregiver? How does the caregiver treat other parents?

- Caregivers encourage parents to visit any time.
- Caregivers are willing to answer parents' questions or talk about the program.
- Caregivers agree with you about discipline, child management.

Individual child. You know your child better than anyone else does. What special qualities, needs, or interests does he or she have that should be taken into consideration in choosing a daycare setting? You should think about this before you visit the center or daycare home. Then, while you are there, pick out a child who seems most like yours. Watch what happens to him or her. Ask the caregiver about special allowances that are made for individual differences in children's naptimes, appetites, activity levels, and so on. List the special qualities and considerations for your child here. For example:

- Active child: there are opportunities to run around freely.
- Child who never naps: center allows child to look at books during naptime or to play in another room.
- Sensitive child, easily overstimulated: daycare facility is quiet, small, perhaps in a home.

Ensuring Continued Quality

Selecting the setting, even after extensive assessment and careful deliberation, is only the first step in ensuring daycare quality. The parents' task is not yet done, and further steps are necessary to see that what looks like good daycare really turns out to be so. Enrolling the child in daycare is not like parking a car in a garage—you need to stay in touch and be involved. Think of yourself as a partner in the daycare arrangement. Know what's going on in the daycare setting and make suggestions. If your child is difficult or slow to warm up, be sure to warn the staff and work with them to help her adjust.

Preparing the child for daycare. Unless the child is a tiny infant, before enrolling or leaving her in the daycare facility, the first step is to prepare the child for daycare. Plunking a child down in a daycare center on day 1, with no warning or preparation, and leaving her there for eight hours should be avoided at all costs.

The immediate effects of leaving the child in the daycare setting can be especially distressing for very young children who are not used to separations from mother. Separation anxiety—for both children and parents—is normal. From the time the child forms an attachment to the parents, as early as seven months of age, and for some children lasting until the end of the preschool period, it is likely that children will be upset at being left in an unfamiliar setting, with a new person. Their distress can be lessened if you take precautions.[10]

Visit the setting together and talk to your child about what daycare will be like. Give the child some experience with other children (in a playgroup or church school, for instance) before daycare begins. Practice separating, by leaving the child with a babysitter occasionally. Stay with the child in daycare until the setting and caregiver are familiar. Progressively lengthen the time the child is left in daycare over the first few weeks. Let the child keep a security blanket or favorite toy with her at daycare. Have another family member (father, grandmother, sibling) or friend stay with the child in daycare for a while. When you leave, tell the child when you will be back, and encourage the caregiver to remind her of this until you return. Then say goodbye and leave without looking back. Do not hover around the door or peek in the window to see how the child is doing. Telephone later to see how things are going.

Older children may not be so distressed at the separation and the newness of daycare, but they need reassurance that they will like the program and that they will get to know the other kids. Shy children need even more time to adjust. All children need regularity and routine in adjusting to daycare. This is not a time to try out new things at home, move to a new house, get a new dog, or take in a boarder. It will be easier for the child if you keep other things at home the same.

Monitoring the caregiver's behavior. As you are easing a child into daycare, you must also be evaluating the quality of the care your child is receiving. Even though you chose the facility because the caregiver passed the test of giving good care to other children, what matters most is what she does for *your* child. When you first bring the child in, introduce the two of them and then let the caregiver take over. Watch carefully what she does. Is she friendly, gentle, welcoming, playful? Continue to keep an eye on her behavior and talk things over with her regularly. Develop a good relationship with the care provider—ask her advice, ask her questions, spend time there. Communication with the caregiver is difficult—in fact, it rarely occurs—but important nonetheless. The child should be the focus of regular, if not daily, conversation. The parent should encourage the caregiver to tell her what the child did that day and should inform her of his behavior and events at home. You should keep the care provider informed of any trouble at home so that she can better support the child at daycare. Talk to the caregiver so that you understand her goals and desires and her "hidden agenda." It might be valuable to invite the caregiver to visit the child at home. It could also be useful for the parent to get active in center activities—building up a library, giving a guest lesson, bringing cookies—just to keep the lines of communication open and to keep a concerned eye on caregiver and child.

Monitoring the child's progress. While the child is in daycare, visit the facility regularly to check whether the child is happy and involved, forming friends, developing social skills. Find time to spend with the child at the center, for both your sakes. At the same time, monitor the child's health and behavior at home. Watch for any new problems—crankiness, sadness, apathy, tantrums, nightmares, bedwetting, loss of appetite, trouble falling asleep, avoidance when you pick him up, defiance, aggression to siblings. Look for warning signs of sexual abuse, such as genital irritation, pain or itching, unusual sexual knowledge, fear of going to daycare, sexual behavior. Look for signs of physical abuse or neglect: bruises, cuts, anxiety, sleep disturbances, nail biting, loss of appetite, a bald patch on the back of the head from spending the day in an infant seat, reluctance to be dropped off, apathy when it's time to go home. Expect some regression at first. It's a big change for the child to adjust to a whole new culture. Be patient and reassuring. But if things don't improve, you may need to find a more suitable daycare arrangement. Compare your child's developmental progress with that of other children the same age. Make sure he isn't falling behind. Talk to the care provider if you are concerned about the child's behavior. The child may be in daycare for eight hours a day, but you are still the parent; what happens in daycare is your responsibility.

Making quality time at home. What happens at home is also your responsibility. You will have less time to spend with the child if you are working full time and the child is in daycare, so make the time you are together count. Make it quality time. Don't be afraid to form a close relationship with the child in order to make separation less painful. The child in daycare needs to be assured that you are there, warm and loving, reliable and responsive, even more than the child who is home all day.

Keeping the status quo. Stability and consistency of care are important for the child; too many changes can disrupt development. But if the parent or the child is unhappy with the arrangement, a change is better than continued irritation. Before the change, it is important again to ensure that the child be prepared and that the next setting or caregiver is more carefully screened.

Active advocacy for daycare. Finally, to improve the quality of daycare for all children, parents can become active advocates for daycare beyond their own immediate needs—joining parents' groups, lobbying, involving the media, schools, churches, and community organizations, speaking out for licensing, research, and new models of daycare, donating their toys, time, and materials. Only by being informed and active can parents and professionals help to ensure that daycare now and for continued generations of children will be the best our society can provide. For daycare is not only a problem for individual parents; it is a problem for society. In the next chapter, we examine the ways in which some other societies have responded to the need for daycare.

10/ Alternatives

In this book so far I have focused on daycare in the United States, where solutions to the problem of finding high-quality daycare are makeshift at best. In many other countries, though, it is not so difficult to find childcare services that are widely available and well organized. It is ironic that although research on children is more extensive and more sophisticated in the United States than in any other country, and although American policymakers have access to more and better information about the factors known to enhance or impede children's development, the United States lags behind almost all other industrialized countries in the supply, quality, and affordability of daycare. The United States, alone with South Africa among advanced industrialized nations, has no clear and integrated national policy to provide support and services for children and families. For this reason, it is instructive to take a look at childcare in some of these other countries to see the variety of solutions they have found to their needs for daycare.[1]

In countries that do have clearly articulated family policies, daycare and preschool programs are thought of as essential components. In France and Belgium, for instance, preschool is a legal "right" or entitlement, as accessible and available as primary school. In Sweden and Finland, childcare for children of working parents is available for all who need it. Countries as diverse as Japan and the Netherlands now have extensive programs for four-year-olds, and many are expanding their coverage for three-year-olds. In addition, almost all civilized countries offer maternity or parenting leaves to permit working women to recover from childbirth and to enable the family to adapt to a new baby. At least two or three months of paid maternal or paternal care is assured in these countries, and often as much as five or six months. In Canada, to name a close neighbor of the United States, employed new mothers have the right to seventeen weeks of leave, paid for through unemployment insurance for fifteen weeks at a rate of 60 percent of the woman's wages. In France, employed women are guaranteed a sixteen-week, job-protected maternity leave, paid for under sickness benefits, and receive about 90 percent of their wages, up to a specified maximum, during this period. A longer leave is permitted and paid for if the child is a third or later-born child, if twins or triplets are born, or if the birth is complicated. In the following pages we will look at the variety of childcare and family services available in some of these other countries, to see if we can learn anything from their experiences.

France

France has a long tradition of public involvement in childcare. In fact, daycare actually began there. In 1799 Johann Oberlin, a Protestant minister, was prodded by his maidservant, Louise Sheppler, into opening the first day nursery, in Alsace. It was a response to the plight of children left on their own while their mothers worked in the fields. The first *crèche* (infant day nursery) opened in

Paris in 1844, again for the benefit of children whose mothers worked. Today in France, daycare for children of working mothers is provided in crèches for infants from six weeks to three years and in *écoles maternelles* for children from two-and-a-half or three to six years. Twenty percent of all infants are in crèches; 90 percent of all two-and-a-half to six-year-olds are in écoles maternelles. Both operate full-day programs, but most infants attend only for part of the day.

Crèches emphasize physical care, health, safety, cleanliness, and motor development and are staffed by "nurses" (secondary-school graduates with two years of vocational training). Since there are not enough places available for all families who want them, priority is given to single parents or families with problems. Crèches are government-approved and subsidized, but a fee on a sliding scale is charged. The larger crèches, with 40 to 60 children, are located in buildings with a courtyard or garden, and the crèche director has an apartment in the building. Smaller crèches, with up to 15 children, are located in houses or apartments. Most other children of working mothers are in family daycare *(crèches familiales)*, some of which are government-run and some, private. In those run by the government, there are no more than three preschool children, including the childcare provider's own.

Ecoles maternelles are like nursery schools in the United States, except they are free. They are basically educational, emphasize social and cognitive development, and are staffed by teachers. They are located near schools. They differ from American nursery schools only in that they operate longer hours: from 9:00 to noon (or 8:00 to 1:00) and 1:00 to 4:00 or 4:30, with a supervised meal period for children who can't go home for lunch and supervised after-school care for children whose parents can't pick them up till later. Parents pay only for lunch and the after-school program.

Although the French regard these programs highly, class sizes are larger than those recommended in the United States. Classes usually have 25 to 35 children with one teacher and sometimes an assistant. French researchers have found, however, that the children who participate in the programs have advantages when they start primary school, just as American children do who attend nursery school. This may be because of the training of the French teachers. Directors of écoles maternelles must be doctors or nurses who have worked for at least five years in the profession, and each school must have a teacher trained in a special college whose task it is to stimulate the children's psychological and emotional development.

Italy

Italy also has a long history of involvement in childcare. But there the issue has not only been whether the government should provide funds for childcare but whether it should be involved in determining what goes on in those programs. For many years, childcare was a political and ideological battleground in Italy, with repeated fights between the Vatican and the state over government involvement in preschool education. But finally, with legislation in 1968 and 1969, the government's right to be directly involved in preprimary education was recognized (Law 444) and "Guidelines for Educational Activities in State Nursery Schools" were approved. This legislation recommended that nursery-school teachers be exclusively women, with either a diploma from a secondary school that trains preschool teachers or an elementary-school teaching certificate. It specified the aims of nursery schools, including educational activities in religion, social interaction, play, language, art, music, and physical development, taking into consideration the most advanced research on early childhood education available at the time. Both state-run and private nursery schools were put under the supervision of the Ministry of Education.

Since the legislation was enacted, there has been a steady increase in the availability and the quality of preschool facilities. Today, there are day nurseries (*asili nili*) for children from birth to three years and nursery schools (*scuole materne*) for children from three to six. Attendance is free and voluntary. Close to 90 percent of three- to five-year-old children attend a preschool, two thirds of which are open eight to ten hours a day, six days a week; most children attend the full-day program. Classes are limited to 15 to 30 children, and the teacher-child ratios have improved substantially since the legislation. In 1968, the teacher-child ratio was 1:24; in 1981, it was 1:12.

Of course these two pieces of legislation did not solve all the issues of childcare. The curricular guidelines they provided were vague, and most were never implemented. The teacher training they recommended turned out to be insufficient; it was either too old-fashioned or too quick and shallow. Both teachers and educational theorists increasingly called for an improved system of basic teacher training that would involve university education. Progress continued to be made, as a result of Italy's commitment to providing better care for children. In 1977, a government decree introduced "experimentation" into the schools, encouraging teachers to conduct research on new teaching methods and models. Such experiments have been particularly notable among communal nursery schools in north-central Italy. There teachers and researchers have come up with new and exciting proposals for the education and care of young children, proposals that are progressive both educationally and socially. A recent issue of *Newsweek* (December 1, 1991), reporting the results of an international search for the best schools in the world, identified this region of Italy as the place to find the best preschools. Clearly government involvement is having a positive effect on the quality of childcare in Italy.

Spain

In Spain maternal employment is relatively rare. Only about a quarter of the mothers of preschool children work. Families also are stable; over 90 percent are two-parent households. Parental-leave policies are generous—new mothers get fourteen weeks of maternity leave and a breastfeeding leave of one hour a day for the first nine months—and parents are entitled to a shorter workday as long as their children are under six years. As a result, Spanish mothers are much involved in childcare, and the government is not.

Another result is that childcare outside the family is not of uniformly high quality. In Spain, setting up a daycare center is easier than setting up a butcher shop or a bar in terms of satisfying licensing requirements. There are no restrictions on staff qualifications, adult-child ratios, or any other aspects of the program. The childcare system is decentralized, and the quality of care varies greatly from one community to another. A wide range of programs exists, from worthwhile to deplorable.

For four- to six-year-olds, there are state-run kindergartens *(jardins de infancia),* and most children attend for part of the day. These kindergartens get standard equipment from the Ministry of Education and Science (carpets, mats, building blocks, symbolic toys, books, flash cards, puppets, paints, hoops, skipping ropes, balls, tricycles, skates, water trays, sand trays, swings, slides, climbing frames) but are given no prescriptive guidelines as to their use. For children under four, as in the United States, there are few government-run programs and the system of childcare is chaotic, with makeshift arrangements. There are only a few daycare centers (*centros de atencion externa*) provided by the Ministry of Education and Science, and another few at workplaces. Most daycare centers or nursery schools (*guarderias*) for children aged two to four are run by private individuals or the Roman Catholic church.

In addition, some working mothers use the equivalent of family daycare, *escuelas di amigas.* Since the sixteenth century, these *migas* or "friendly women" have been the major source of childcare for children of working mothers. They not only cared for the children but also prayed aloud with them and taught them to read and write, collecting a meager payment each day as they inspected the children's hands for cleanliness.

Spain provides an example of what happens in a country in which the demand for childcare is not great, the childcare system is decentralized, and the government is not actively involved.

Sweden

In Sweden, in contrast, the government takes a particularly active role in providing services for all citizens, from birth to old age. The social-security system covers childbirth, health, education, and family support. Childrearing is considered a responsibility to be shared by parents and society. Thus the Swedish solution to the problem posed by working mothers includes lengthy paid maternity and paternity leaves, paid leaves for a parent when a child is sick, a reduced workweek for both parents (six hours a day until the child is eight years old), and government-run childcare. Daycare is considered a right of all children and particularly important for those who require special support for their development.

Employed parents—mothers or fathers—can take a job-protected leave for fifteen months after the birth of a baby and, for twelve of those months, receive a cash benefit equal to 90 percent of their earnings. In later 1992 the government plans to extend paid parental leave to eighteen months. At present, a working mother can take off six months, and then she and her husband can each work half time for nine months, sharing childcare between them. Or a mother and a father can each work three quarters of the time for one year. What usually happens is that the mother takes an equivalent of about eight and a half months, the father one and a half months. Any of these options can be taken without significant pay loss.

After the maternity or paternity leaves are over, daycare centers (*daghems*) provide care for children from six months to seven years, offering either full- or part-time care, whichever the parents want. There are few private daycare centers; even parent cooperatives and church centers get public funds. But although all programs are heavily subsidized, parents do pay some fees, in proportion to their incomes, usually amounting to less than 10 percent of the woman's wages.

Daycare centers in Sweden are of uniformly high quality, spacious, well-equipped, educational, and located in buildings specifically designed for that purpose. Their staffs include teachers, nurses, and instructors in childcare. All staff working with children under three years must be specially trained as children's nurses or preschool teachers. Staff-child ratios are high—four staff members for every ten to twelve toddlers or fifteen preschoolers. These standards for staff-child ratios and caregiver qualifications are based on extensive research and rigorously set and enforced.

Even in Sweden, however, since the proportion of working mothers with young children is so high (80 percent), the demand for center spaces exceeds the supply, so licensed daycare homes *(familjedaghem)* are also used. These homes are organized so that the municipality pays the care providers directly and parents pay the municipality. Care providers receive a fixed monthly salary if they look after the equivalent of at least four children full time. In later 1992, the Swedish government has announced, all children over one and a half years are to be guaranteed a place in a center.

Russia

Like Sweden, the former Soviet Union had a socialist family policy, which offered an extensive system of health care and social services. Since it was essential for the economy of the nation that mothers work, the Soviets instituted the most extensive program of group upbringing in human history. Although mothers could take up to a year's maternity leave, they usually returned to work much sooner. The Soviet daycare program encouraged group care because of the communist notion that children are to be brought up "in the collective, by the collective, and for the collective." It was started under Khrushchev in 1956 and became a highly centralized and sophisticated system of state-run *yasli-sads* (nurseries and kindergartens).

Children were still likely to be cared for by a *babushka* (grandmother) in their infancy, but, lacking a babushka, the state nurseries were available from six weeks on. By the time they were two or three, most children were in these nurseries; at four years they went to a state kindergarten. Statistics have been hard to obtain, but it is estimated that the number of children in full-time care in these nurseries and kindergartens ranged from 20 percent of the three- to seven-year-olds in rural areas to 75 percent of the three- to seven-year-olds in the cities. In Moscow in the late 1980s, there were over 3,000 yaslisads. What will happen to daycare in the new Commonwealth of Independent States now that democracy and free enterprise are replacing the communist system will be interesting to watch. Mothers may soon find that in addition to their other problems—such as standing in long lines for scarce food they can't afford—they will have to pay for daycare themselves. Or perhaps, because they have seen its value, the people will not allow state-supported daycare to disappear.

The programs in the Soviet nurseries and kindergartens, both under the Ministry of Education, were perhaps the most highly developed and uniform in the world. The curriculum was based on early childhood research and emphasized industriousness, aesthetics, character, cooperation, group awareness, problem solving, and creativity. Although there was time for children to indulge in role play, games of stimulation and physical exercise, gymnastics, and music, nothing was left to chance in this curriculum; everything was planned and specified— even the temperature—and spontaneous play only occurred at prescribed times and places, directed by nurse-upbringers who had three years of training at a teachers' college. Cooperation and helping were strongly encouraged: children were placed together in playpens at an early age, and all toys belonged to the group, not to individuals. The children learned early that "what's mine is ours; what's ours is mine." As soon as they could talk, children were also given training in evaluating and criticizing each other's behaviors from the point of view of the group.

The following excerpt from the manual that all nurse-upbringers followed illustrates the specificity of the curriculum.[2] This is an example of a lesson to be given during the second and third years.

Activity with spherical objects

Goal: To acquaint children with the characteristics of spherical objects and basic colors.

A toy bowling alley (40 cm. long, 10 cm. wide, 15 cm. high, and with sides 2–3 cm. high) is used. Also a medium-sized box which contains small wooden balls of four colors (red, blue, yellow, and green). There should be two balls of each color.

Procedure: Six children are seated in a semicircle, the adult facing them. The "bowling alley" is put in such a position that the balls roll toward the children. The adult shows how one rolls the balls. She says: "Children, I have some balls in my box. Look how beautiful they are." She shows them red balls and places them in their hands. "I'll roll the red ball. It rolls this way. It rolled to Natasha. Natasha, please bring me the red ball. It rolled to Yura. Yura, please bring the red ball and put it in the box. Natasha, sit on your chair." In this way she shows blue, yellow, and green balls. Then she says: "Roll the yellow ball. Natasha, please bring me the yellow ball. Take the same ball and roll it in the bowling alley." The children bring the balls, take them out of the box and roll them.

China

China also has an extensive system of nurseries, although it is less extensive than what was found in the Soviet Union and differs considerably in content. For one thing, it is more casual. The Soviet upbringer had three years of professional school; the Chinese "auntie" may be chosen for childcare because she is patient and responsible; she is not likely to have completed high school. The Chinese nursery for infants up to age three is usually located in the factory so that the mother can come by to nurse her infant. Children are in small groups (six or seven) of same-age peers with one auntie. The youngest infants (two to eight months) are put in pairs in playpens or carriages; there is no attempt by the auntie to "stimulate" them. When they are old enough, the infants sit together in a circle and play group games, in an orderly manner, or perform songs and dances. Infants are not encouraged to walk, crawl, play alone, or explore materials; their activities are social and artistic, not cognitive or academic.

After age three, the children go to kindergarten (up to age seven). Here activities become structured and regulated. There are toys and educational materials, but no science materials, table games, blocks, dramatic play props, or picture books as one might find in a western nursery school or kindergarten. The curriculum consists of language and politics, mathematics, group recitation, song and dance, drawing and painting, physical training and hygiene, moral character, general knowledge, and productive labor. The daily routine is specified in "Regulations" (written in 1952) to include: opening at 7:00 a.m.; breakfast; activity periods; play; lunch; nap; snack; play; dinner; dismissal at 6:30 p.m. There is no free choice or creative problem-solving activity. On average, one teacher has responsibility for a class of 27.

All activities in kindergarten are geared toward the goals of work and serving others. These kindergartens were set up and have continued to grow in number ever since the founding of the People's Republic of China in

1949. Their purpose is to foster children's healthy development before primary school as well as to lighten mothers' childcare burdens so that they can take part in political, cultural, and educational activities. The kindergartens are run by factories, the army, governmental and academic institutions, the national Board of Education, and local neighborhoods, towns, villages, and private individuals. About 20 percent of the three- to six-year-old children attend kindergarten. They may attend either part time or full days. They may even board at the kindergarten and stay all week except Sunday. A boarding kindergarten may have over 100 children and has a doctor and nurse on staff.

Israel

The Israeli kibbutz offers a very different childcare arrangement, also based on communal ideology and a national need for all citizens, including women, to work. In most kibbutzim the children live in a Children's House rather than with their own families. There they spend their time in a social unit of four or five other children of the same age, under the supervision of a *metapelet*. Each unit has its own bedroom, bathroom, diningroom, playroom, and yard. At first, when children are only infants, mothers spend time with them and the metaplot in the Infants' House. But after the first year, children go to the Toddlers' House and then to the Children's House. There they usually see their parents and siblings only for two hours in the late afternoon when the family gets together in the parents' quarters. These visits with the parents are purely social; instruction, discipline, and physical caregiving are taken care of in the Children's House. Parents may visit children at the house at other times and are encouraged to do so for their own emotional satisfaction, but visits are supposed to be brief with no disruption of the child's routine. The parent can participate in the ongoing activity, but should not interfere with or comment on the work of the metapelet.

Metaplot are selected as teenagers after they demonstrate an aptitude for childcare by helping in the Children's House. They are trained and follow a manual that contains specific instructions for their work—including how to relate to the mother, how to toilet-train the child, what table manners to instill, and how to read stories.[3] They are solely responsible for dressing, supervising, and training "their" youngsters. When children are four to seven years old, the metapelet assists a teacher in giving a larger group of children lessons in science, art, and nature. Since it is believed that children must grow to depend on themselves, the metapelet encourages independence by leaving the children alone together for long periods.

The effects of this dramatically different form of child-rearing have been studied in Israel, by comparing the development of kibbutz children with that of other Israeli children raised in traditional families with greater participation in care by their parents (including children in a *moshav*, a community with the same cooperative ideology but a traditional family structure).[4] These studies show no differences in mental development or mental health, but there are some differences in the qualities of the children's relationships with family and friends. Kibbutz children do form strong, positive relationships with their mothers, siblings, and friends, just as children in more traditional family arrangements do, but their feelings—both positive and negative—in the relationships are more moderate and not so focused on single individuals. They diffuse their affection across a larger number of people, and their relations with any of them are less intimate. They see their parents as nurturant and supportive but at the same time encouraging of independence; their peers are seen as supportive, but the friendships are less intense. In addition to this difference in the intensity of interpersonal relations, kibbutz children are able earlier to approach and be sociable to unfamiliar children, to see another person's point of view, and to cooperate in group activities.

This quick trip around the world reveals profound differences in the ways children are raised and cared for. Sometimes Americans act as if the way we do it here is the only way. Clearly it is not, and we can certainly get some good ideas about childcare from other countries.

11 / The Future

It is clear that, for the foreseeable future at least, daycare is here to stay. It is part of modern life. In the next ten years, daycare in the United States will probably increase in scope and scale. It *could* also improve in quality. In this final chapter I suggest a few of the things that might make parents' lives easier and daycare better in the next decade.

New Information

In the next ten years, we may learn more about the effects of daycare on children's development from several large-scale studies that have just begun. In the Study of Early Child Care sponsored by the National Institute of Child Health and Human Development, a cohort of children has been identified and is being studied from birth through their first three years (possibly longer). They are observed periodically at home and in any regular day-care arrangements in which they spend at least ten hours a week. Their experiences at home and in daycare will then be related to their cognitive, social, and emotional development, assessed using a variety of standard and original instruments. Some 1,200 infants, from a wide range of family backgrounds in ten different sites across the country, are being studied. In the Child and Family Study being conducted by ChildTrends and the Manpower Demonstration Research Corporation, the effects of one year of daycare on children whose welfare mothers are randomly assigned to the Job Opportunity and Basic Skills Training (JOBS) program are being studied. The cognitive, physical, emotional, and social development of 2,500 three- to five-year-olds is being studied over a five-year period. In a third study, the Expanded Childcare Options (ECCO) demonstration project funded by the Rockefeller Foundation, the development of 1,800 children is being assessed, beginning in early childhood and extending into young adulthood. The purpose of this study is to compare the effects of basic daycare (one year), extended daycare (lasting until first grade), and extended enhanced daycare (high-quality care lasting until first grade). Welfare mothers with a child under three years are randomly assigned to one of these conditions.

Because of their scope and design, these projects promise to yield important data on the effects of daycare on children's behavior and development. They are the most significant and substantial studies of daycare ever undertaken. They will include more detailed assessments of how well children are doing and more detailed observations of the quality of their daycare than has been possible before. They will answer specific questions about what kinds of daycare are acceptable and what kinds of daycare arrangements are optimal (daycare in a home or a center, daycare for 25 hours a week or 35, and so on).

Changes in Work Patterns

In the next decade we may also see changes in the ways people work, changes that will affect the kinds of daycare they need. More people will be able to work at home, connected to the workplace by computer, modem, and electronic mail. Parents working at home would be able to use an in-home care provider who is not professionally trained, since they would still be in the house to provide overall supervision and consultation. They could also schedule some of their worktime to coincide with youngster's naps and favorite TV shows, and so they would need to pay for fewer hours of a care provider's time.

Another change in work schedules might be that more parents could find part-time work and shared jobs. In the United States, the vast majority of people who are employed are employed full time. In a survey conducted by General Mills, however, 42 percent of the respondents felt that part-time work with full-time benefits would help a great deal in reducing the tensions caused by balancing work and family demands.[1] Some organizations are considering transitional part-time work at least for the period when employees are parents with young children. In other countries, such as Great Britain, part-time work is the norm for mothers of preschool children. If part-time work were more common here, this would help both working parents and their children. Parents would not be so overburdened and stressed by their double load. Daycare would be more readily available because part-time programs would be sufficient. Children would benefit from having the enrichment of a part-time daycare experience and still have a good deal of time at home.

One possible solution to the need for full-time work and full-time parenting is "flexitime." This has been suggested as a way of freeing working parents—both fathers and mothers—for childcare. In the flexitime system, employees can tailor their work schedules to their family schedules. They are required to maintain certain core hours at the job, but they can arrive and depart at different times. Couples can maximize the time that one or the other parent can be home with the children, so they would not need to use as much daycare.

Maternity leaves from work, after the birth of an infant, are another change that could make parents' lives easier. In the United States some limited maternity leaves are provided through disability benefits. The Pregnancy Discrimination Act of 1978 determined that pregnancy must be treated like any other worker disability. That is, if a corporation provides disability benefits, pregnant women must be included; their jobs must be protected. But only 40 percent of all working women are covered by maternity-leave benefits,[2] and the length of time they are allowed is usually only six to eight weeks, sometimes as little as four weeks. If women were allowed longer leaves, including both paid and unpaid time, with guaranteed job security and no loss of seniority, it would not be necessary for infants to be in daycare for the first several months of their lives.

Paternity leaves are also possible. In some countries, fathers are also offered a leave of absence from the job for several months after the birth of the baby. In the United States few companies offer paternity leaves except informally through sick days, vacation, or unpaid leaves. Although it is unlikely that we will see an increase in paternity-leave policies over the next decade, this might be a way of eventually reducing the pressure on mothers.

Improvements in Daycare

In addition to these changes in employment policies, the next ten years may see increases in daycare accessibility.

One way that daycare may become more accessible is through an increase in resource and referral services. These services can be provided by city governments, by private individuals, or by corporations. In fact, this was the fastest-growing corporate childcare initiative in the 1980s, as companies realized that "R & R" was a low-cost employment benefit. Resource and referral services offer counseling to help parents make daycare choices and may also provide money or resources to increase the quantity or improve the quality of daycare. Parents phone or visit an R & R service when they are first thinking about childcare. They are interviewed about the kind, location, and cost of daycare desired. Then the R & R staff provides a list of options that fit the parents' criteria. They do not recommend one program over another, but they may give parents guidelines for making a choice. In 1984, IBM offered R & R services to its 220,000 employees in the United States. They retained a private firm of consultants to coordinate a national network of R & R agencies and to increase the quantity of daycare in all their sites throughout the country. They have been quite successful in expanding the supply of daycare as well as building a national network of R & R services.

Some corporations also support community daycare, paying for "slots" for their employees' children, and a few actually provide on-site care. Employers report that this improves their employees' morale, attracts talented workers, and serves as good public relations. It also reduces employee turnover and thus improves the company's productivity.[3] The number of employers getting involved in daycare is growing—although it is still extremely small—and we might expect that increase to continue over the next ten years. One employer with an innovative idea is Stride Rite Shoes: they have a center in which daycare for the young is combined with day-care for the elderly.

Another increase in daycare availability might result from increased involvement by schools. So-called "new schools of the 21st century" would offer daycare in school buildings, administered through the school system, with satellite networks of all the daycare homes in the neighborhood, and accompanied by parent-education outreach programs. These school-based daycare centers would be staffed by personnel with degrees in early childhood education or child development, not by elementary schoolteachers. They would offer a balance of academic and nonacademic activities, not simply an extension of the elementary curriculum downward.

This idea of using schools has several justifications. Schools are one of the most reliable, permanent, and stable institutions in our society. Their existence is not contingent on finding new funding from year to year. For another thing, schools could offer equal access to daycare for all children who need it, because they are open to all children. Additionally, schools have as their goal the optimal development of children, not the goal of allowing parents to work or the goal of helping the needy. Being part of the public-school system would remove the stigma from daycare and would provide a more suitable goal for daycare services—promoting children's well-being. As part of the school system, daycare would be a "right" for all citizens rather than a service for the poor or a luxury for the affluent. Finally, tying daycare to the schools could upgrade its quality. Teachers are better paid than daycare workers, and daycare workers in school-based programs are the most highly educated and well paid in the field. Having daycare in the schools could lead to upgrading childcare as a profession and improving the salaries of childcare workers. Bills proposing such new schools have been placed before Congress, and some states already have them. We might expect an expansion of daycare in this direction over the next decade.

Of course there are concerns about tying daycare to the schools. Perhaps daycare would become too academic—a fear that is justified by seeing how school-like our kindergartens are. There are also concerns that removing preschoolers from home care would make that form of daycare unavailable to infants and toddlers, since a caregiver can care for fewer infants and toddlers than she can for preschoolers. But most people agree that if the United States is to have an adequate system of childcare, schools will have to play a large part. They are the only institution with the societal mission and potential capacity to provide universal childcare.

Another change we might witness in the coming decade is an increase in the regulation of daycare by the federal government, a change that might eliminate inadequate care in states with excessively low standards. Across the states, for example, adult-child ratios range from 1:3 to 1:8 for infants, from 1:5 to 1:20 for preschoolers. These ratios reflect substantially different levels of quality and at the low end undoubtedly reflect poor care. In the Child Care Staffing study, for instance, it was found that many more of the children in the states with the least stringent childcare regulations (Georgia, Arizona) were in poor-quality care than in states with more stringent regulations (Massachusetts, Washington).[4] In Georgia, only 2 percent of the centers observed met the FIDCR standards, whereas in Massachusetts nearly half did. In Georgia, the infants and younger toddlers in the study spent more than half of the observation periods in aimless wandering; older toddlers and preschoolers spent close to one third of the time wandering. Only 18 percent of the young toddlers, 29 percent of the older toddlers, and 8 percent of the preschoolers demonstrated age-appropriate behavior with peers; only 42 percent received average or higher scores on intelligence tests.

Clearly, governmental regulation cannot create or guarantee high-quality care. But research shows that unregulated daycare is of lower quality than regulated care, and daycare quality is higher in states with tighter regulations.[5] This does seem to suggest that regulation could help to eliminate inadequate care. Setting a floor for quality that all states could agree on could lead to better and more equitable daycare. Federal or state regulation could establish minimal adult-child ratios of 1:4 for infants and 1:10 for preschoolers and minimal levels of training for caregivers, and this would do much to improve the quality of existing care. The attention given to legislation, such as the ABC Bill discussed earlier, suggests that many people feel the need for such regulation.

Some policymakers have expressed concern, however, that governmental regulation would increase daycare costs. They worry particularly about the cost of home daycare, which is all that many families can afford. But regulation need not increase the cost of care provided by friends or neighbors. Daycare providers who offer inexpensive home care are not in the childcare business to make a lot of money. If daycare were regulated so that the home care provider took in fewer children, or if she were told how to increase the safety of her home by turning in pot handles on the stove and barricading the stairs, or if she could learn a bit more about how to play with young children or how to reduce children's aggression by teaching them social skills, regulation would not increase the cost to the parents or the government. Regulations that required expensive physical changes to daycare homes or enrollment in community college courses could be adjusted to keep daycare costs down. Training of care providers could be accomplished economically by means of community TV or coordination with organized daycare networks or playground programs. If the purpose of regulation were to identify a reasonable *floor* of quality and to eliminate or modify care that fell below that level, the enforcement of regulations might be more feasible and daycare costs would not increase. Regulation could at least serve to prevent the warehousing of large groups of children in unsafe and unstimulating facilities.

Organizing home daycare into networks is another idea that may become more popular in the 1990s. In 1978, it was estimated that 30,000 daycare home providers were in networks; in 1986, 85,000 were. This increase was largely the result of state or local requirements governing federal subsidies under social security for children from low-income families. The services provided by networks include referrals, caregiver training, toy lending libraries, technical assistance, shared activities, drop-in centers, and emergency back-up caregivers. Daycare providers in networks have been observed to offer better care than licensed care providers who are not in networks. If the number of networks continues to increase, this too could improve daycare quality. It would also probably improve quality if both daycare centers and homes were included in the networks, rather than just homes.

Lessons from Abroad

In the last chapter we had a hint of the great variation that exists in daycare around the world. The need for daycare is felt everywhere. Yet in almost all other countries more concerted efforts have been made to provide care for all who need it. Perhaps the 1990s will also be the time to learn some lessons from abroad.

One thing we could do would be to extend the length of the day in existing nursery-school arrangements, to make them more like the French écoles maternelles. This would increase the value of existing centers so that they could be used for daycare by full-time working parents as well as for providing part-time educational enrichment. Another measure would be to set up separate daycare facilities for infants and toddlers, as in France, China, and Israel. This would require support from the government, in this country too, because infants require so much adult attention that it is difficult to provide affordable care for infants in centers. We could also encourage a more explicitly educational curriculum in daycare. Of course the curriculum in the United States would be based on different values, stressing verbal skills, artistic expression, social competence, independence and free choice, not taken from the manuals of the Soviet nurse-upbringers or the Israeli metaplot. The idea of having a tightly standardized curriculum would probably never be accepted here, where diversity is so highly valued. But a variety of educational packages could be published and promoted.

Another idea from abroad would be to select daycare providers on the basis of aptitude, like the Israeli metapelet or the Chinese auntie, rather than simply on the basis of educational credentials. These caregivers, who might or might not have college degrees, would then be trained in child development and early childhood education. This training could be offered on the job to those who had shown an aptitude for caregiving, rather than as a college course taken before applying for a childcare position. Working in the daycare facility, these caregivers could then be offered ongoing consultation with expert advisers, as in Sweden. There could also be more systematic, if not centralized, supervision of daycare facilities, as occurs in most of the countries we looked at. Finally, we could integrate daycare into a larger system of family and childcare supports, as also has been done elsewhere.

It is wishful thinking to expect that daycare is bound to improve over the next ten or twenty or even fifty years. It is just as likely that it will get worse. Certainly we have seen over the past decade that, although daycare has become more available, much of it has decreased in quality. Facilities have expanded and stretched to take in more and more children, but they have not hired more caregivers with better training and paid them higher wages. In this chapter I have suggested some ways that daycare and parents' plight could improve. It requires a great deal of effort. Making that effort, though, will be worthwhile in the end. Only then will our children receive the kind of care they—and we—need and deserve.

Notes

1 / THE PROBLEM

1. J. P. Robinson, J. Yerby, M. Fieweger, and N. Somerick, "Sex-Role Differences in Time Use," *Sex Roles*, 3 (1977), 443–458. K. E. Walker and M. E. Woods, "Time Use for Care of Family Members," Use-of-Time Research Project, Human Ecology, Cornell University, Working Paper No. 1 (September 1972).
2. E. Galinsky, "Family Life and Corporate Policies," in M. W. Yogman and T. B. Brazelton, eds., *In Support of Families* (Cambridge: Harvard University Press, 1986).
3. For example, J. Curtis, *Working Mothers* (New York: Doubleday, 1976). E. Thomopoulos and H. M. Huyck, paper presented at annual convention of the American Psychological Association, Washington, D.C., 1976. S. Welch and A. Booth, "Employment and Health among Married Women with Children," *Sex Roles*, 3 (1977), 385–397. L. W. Hoffman, "Effect of Maternal Employment on the Child," *Child Development*, 32 (1961), 187–197. L. W. Hoffman, "Maternal Employment and the Young Child," in M. Perlmutter, ed., *Parent-Child Interaction and Parent-Child Relations in Child Development* (Hillsdale: Erlbaum, 1984).
4. K. Keniston and the Carnegie Council on Children, *All Our Children* (New York: Harcourt Brace Jovanovich, 1977).
5. Yankelovich, Skelly and White, Inc., *Raising Children in a*

175

Changing Society, General Mills American Family Report, 1976–77 (Minneapolis: General Mills, 1977), pp. 3–4.

6. G. W. Brown and T. O. Harris, *Social Origins of Depression* (London: Tavistock, 1978).

7. J. E. Harrell and C. A. Ridley, "Substitute Child Care, Maternal Employment and the Quality of Mother-Child Interaction," *Journal of Marriage and the Family,* 37 (1975), 556–564. M. R. Yarrow, P. Scott, L. DeLeeuw, and C. Heinig, "Child-Rearing in Families of Working and Nonworking Mothers," *Sociometry,* 25 (1962), 122–140. Hoffman, "Effect of Maternal Employment." It should be noted that it is not possible to establish from these studies, based on samples in which it was the subject's own choice to work, whether the satisfied mothers would have been satisfied no matter what they were doing (working or not working).

8. A. C. Emlen and P. E. Koren, "Hard to Find and Difficult to Manage: The Effects of Child Care on the Workplace" (Portland: Regional Institute for Human Services, 1984).

9. M. Whitebook, C. Howes, and D. A. Phillips, *Who Cares? Child Care Teachers and the Quality of Care in America. Final Report. National Child Care Staffing Study* (Oakland: Child Care Employee Project, 1989).

10. S. L. Hofferth and D. A. Phillips, "Child Care Policy Research," *Journal of Social Issues,* 47 (1991), 1–13.

2 / NEW NEEDS

1. M. C. Howell, "Employed Mothers and Their Families (1)," *Pediatrics,* 52 (1973), 252–263.

2. S. Yudkin and A. Holme, *Working Mothers and Their Children* (London: Sphere Books, 1969).

3. S. L. Hofferth, "Day Care in the Next Decade: 1980–1990," *Journal of Marriage and the Family,* 41 (1979), 649–658.

4. G. Russell, "The Father Role and Its Relation to Masculinity, Femininity, and Androgyny," *Child Development,* 49 (1978), 1174–81.

5. Reported in *Newsweek,* November 10, 1980, p. 110.

6. J. Kellerman and E. R. Katz, "Attitudes toward the Divi-

sion of Child-Rearing Responsibilities," *Sex Roles,* 4 (1978), 505–512.

7. Walker and Woods, "Time Use for Care of Family Members."

8. H. H. Bohen and A. Viveros-Long, *Balancing Jobs and Family Life* (Philadelphia: Temple University Press, 1981).

9. Yankelovich, Skelly and White, *Raising Children in a Changing Society.*

10. E. E. Kisker, S. L. Hofferth, D. A. Phillips, and E. Farquhar, *A Profile of Child Care Settings: Early Education and Care in 1990,* report prepared for the U.S. Department of Education, contract no. LC88090001 (Washington, D.C., 1991).

11. M. Bone, *Preschool Children and the Need for Day Care* (London: Her Majesty's Stationery Office, Office of Population Censuses and Surveys, Social Survey Division, 1977). Study of Childcare arrangements by Thomas Coram Research Unit, London, 1977.

12. S. Oskamp, *Journal of Social Issues,* 47 (1991).

13. Whitebook et al., *Who Cares?*

14. Kisker et al., *A Profile of Child Care Settings.*

15. D. A. Phillips, C. Howes, and M. Whitebook, "Child Care as an Adult Work Environment," *Journal of Social Issues,* 47 (1991), 49–70. Kisker et al., *A Profile of Child Care Settings.*

3 / HISTORY

1. For documentation and more detail on the history of daycare in the United States, see M. O. Steinfels, *Who's Minding the Children? The History and Politics of Day Care in America* (New York: Simon and Schuster, 1973). N. M. Robinson, H. B. Robinson, M. A. Darling, and G. Holm, *A World of Children: Day Care and Pre-School Institutions* (Monterey: Brooks/Cole, 1979).

4 / HERE AND NOW

1. Dickinson, "Child Care."

2. Kisker et al., *A Profile of Child Care Settings.*

3. A. R. Pence and H. Goelman, "Silent Partners: Parents of Children in Three Types of Day Care," *Early Childhood Research Quarterly,* 2 (1987), 103–118.
4. M. D. Keyserling, *Windows on Day Care: A Report on the Findings of Members of the National Council of Jewish Women on Day Care Needs and Services in Their Communities* (Educational Resources Information Center [ERIC], 1972, ED 063 027). ERIC publications may be obtained from their Document Service, P.O. Box 190, Arlington, Virginia 22210.
5. For example, M. Golden et al., *The New York City Infant Day Care Study* (New York: Medical and Health Association of New York City, 1978). A. C. Emlen et al., *Child Care by Kith: A Study of the Family Day Care Relationships of Working Mothers and Neighborhood Caregivers* (ERIC, 1971, ED 060 955). S. Fosburg et al., *National Day Care Home Study* (Cambridge: Abt Associates, 1980).
6. B. Bryant, M. Harris, and D. Newton, *Children and Minders* (London: Grant McIntyre, 1980), pp. 114–115.
7. For example, Golden et al., *New York City Infant Day Care Study.* B. Tyler and L. Dittmann, "Meeting the Toddler More Than Halfway: The Behavior of Toddlers and Their Caregivers," *Young Children,* January 1980, p. 39. M. M. Cochran, "A Comparison of Group Day and Family Child-Rearing Patterns in Sweden," *Child Development,* 48 (1977), 702–707. E. Prescott, *Group and Family Day Care: A Comparative Assessment* (ERIC, 1972, ED 060 945).

5 / EFFECTS ON CHILDREN

1. Compared to figures in Kisker et al., *Profile of Child Care Settings.*
2. At the Frank Porter Graham Center in North Carolina by C. Ramey, D. Farran, et al., and the Milwaukee Project in Wisconsin by R. Heber and H. Garber.
3. Golden et al., *New York Infant Day Care Study.* C. T. Ramey, D. MacPhee, and K. O. Yeates, "Preventing Developmental Retardation: A General Systems Model," in L. Bond and J. Joffe, eds., *Facilitating Infant and Early Child Care Develop-*

ment (Hanover: University Press of New England, 1982). H. B. Robinson and N. M. Robinson, "Longitudinal Development of Very Young Children in a Comprehensive Day Care Program: The First Two Years," *Child Development,* 42 (1971), 1673–83. K. Vroegh, "Infant Day Care: Some Research Findings," unpublished paper, Institute for Juvenile Research, Chicago (ERIC, 1976, ED 145 968).

4. J. W. B. Douglas and J. M. Blomfield, *Children under Five* (London: Allen and Unwin, 1958). W. Fowler and N. Khan, *The Later Effects of Infant Group Care: A Follow Up Study* (Toronto: Ontario Institute for Studies in Education, 1974). M. E. Keister, *"The Good Life" for Infants and Toddlers* (Washington, D.C.: National Association for the Education of Young Children, 1970).

5. C. D. Hayes, J. L. Palmer, and M. J. Zaslow, eds., *Who Cares for America's Children?* (Washington, D.C.: National Academy Press, 1990).

6. S. S. Aronson, "Health and Safety in Child Care," and E. K. Oremland, "Childhood Illness and Day Care," in S. S. Chehrazi, ed., *Psychosocial Issues in Day Care* (Washington, D.C.: American Psychiatric Press, 1990).

7. D. L. Vandell, V. K. Henderson, and K. S. Wilson, "A Longitudinal Study of Children with Day-Care Experiences of Varying Quality," *Child Development,* 59 (1988), 1286–92. E. C. Melhuish, E. Lloyd, S. Martin, and A. Mooney, "Type of Child Care at 18 Months, II. Relations with Cognitive and Language Development," *Journal of Child Psychology and Psychiatry,* 31 (1990), 861–870. M. V. Peaslee, "The Development of Competency in Two-Year-Old Infants in Day Care and Home Reared Environments," diss., Florida State University, 1976.

8. See J. Belsky, L. D. Steinberg, and A. Walker, "The Ecology of Day Care," in M. E. Lamb, ed., *Childrearing in Nontraditional Families* (Hillsdale: Erlbaum, 1982). K. A. Clarke-Stewart and G. Fein, "Programs for Young Children: Day Care and Early Education," in P. Mussen, M. Haith, and J. Campos, eds., *Handbook of Child Psychology* (New York: Wiley, 1983). Hayes et al., *Who Cares for America's Children?*

B.-E. Andersson, "Effects of Public Day Care: A Longitudinal Study," *Child Development,* 60 (1989), 857–866. M. Burchinal, M. Lee, and C. Ramey, "Type of Day Care and Preschool Intellectual Development in Disadvantaged Children," *Child Development,* 60 (1989), 128–137. Cochran, "A Comparison of Group Day and Family Child-Rearing Patterns in Sweden." W. Fowler, *Day Care and Its Effects on Early Development: A Study of Group and Home Care in Multi-Ethnic, Working-Class Families* (Toronto: Ontario Institute for Studies in Education, 1978). H. Garber and R. Heber, "Modification of Predicted Cognitive Development in High-Risk Children through Early Intervention," paper presented at meeting of the American Educational Research Association, Boston, April 1980; published in *Intelligence,* 4:3 (1980). Golden et al., *New York City Infant Day Care Study.* J. Kagan, R. B. Kearsley, and P. R. Zelazo, *Infancy: Its Place in Human Development* (Cambridge: Harvard University Press, 1978). C. T. Ramey, B. Dorval, and L. Baker-Ward, "Group Day Care and Socially Disadvantaged Families: Effects on the Child and the Family," in S. Kilmer, ed., *Advances in Early Education and Day Care,* vol. 3 (Greenwich: JAI Press, 1983). J. L. Rubenstein and C. Howes, "Social-Emotional Development of Toddlers in Day Care: The Role of Peers and of Individual Differences," in Kilmer, ed., *Advances in Early Education and Day Care.* S. Scarr, J. Lande, and K. McCartney, "Child Care and the Family," in J. Lande, S. Scarr, and N. Gunzenhauser, eds., *Caring for Children: Challenge to America* (Hillsdale: Erlbaum, 1988). R. A. Winnett, W. L. Fuchs, S. Moffatt, and V. J. Nerviano, "A Cross-Sectional Study of Children and Their Families in Different Child Care Environments," *Journal of Community Psychology,* 5 (1977), 149–159. A. Doyle and K. Somers, "The Effects of Group and Family Day Care on Infant Attachment Behaviours," *Canadian Journal of Behavioural Science,* 10 (1978), 38–45. C. T. Ramey and P. J. Mills, "Social and Intellectual Consequences of Day Care for High-Risk Infants," in R. A. Webb, ed., *Social Development in Childhood: Day Care Programs and Research*

(Baltimore: Johns Hopkins University Press, 1977). Robinson and Robinson, "Longitudinal Development of Very Young Children in a Comprehensive Day Care Program." Fowler, *Day Care and Its Effects on Early Development.* Fowler and Khan, *The Later Effects of Infant Group Care.* Golden et al., *New York Infant Day Care Study.* Kagan et al., *Infancy: Its Place in Human Development.* J. L. Rubenstein, C. Howes, and P. Boyle, "A Two-Year Follow-Up of Infants in Community Based Infant Day Care," *Journal of Child Psychology and Psychiatry,* 22 (1981), 209–218.

9. Steinberg and Green, "Three Types of Day Care."
10. For example, Fowler, *Day Care and Its Effects on Early Development.* J. R. Lally and A. S. Honig, "The Family Development Research Program," final report (OCD-CB-100) to the Office of Child Development, Department of Health, Education, and Welfare, April 1977. Ramey et al., "Preventing Developmental Retardation: A General Systems Model." Garber and Heber, "Modification of Predicted Cognitive Development in High-Risk Children through Early Intervention." Fowler and Khan, *Later Effects of Infant Group Care.*
11. A. F. Osborn, and J. E. Milbank, *The Effects of Early Education* (Oxford: Oxford University Press, 1987). S. Jowett and K. Sylva, "Does Kind of Preschool Matter?" *Educational Review,* 28 (1986), 21–31. J. W. Swift, "Effects of Early Group Experience: The Nursery School and Day Nursery," in M. L. Hoffman and L. W. Hoffman, eds., *Review of Child Development Research* (New York: Russell Sage Foundation, 1964).
12. I. Lazar et al., "The Persistence of Preschool Effects: A Long-Term Follow-Up of Fourteen Infant and Preschool Experiments," final report (18–76–07843) to the Administration on Children, Youth, and Families, Office of Human Development Services, Department of Health, Education and Welfare, September 1977.
13. Andersson, "Effects of Public Day Care: A Longitudinal Study." K. A. Clarke-Stewart, "Predicting Child Development from Child Care Forms and Features: The Chicago

Study," in D. A. Phillips, ed., *Quality in Child Care: What Does Research Tell Us?* Research Monographs of the National Association for the Education of Young Children, vol. 1 (Washington, D.C.: NAEYC, 1987). Cochran, "A Comparison of Group Day and Family Child-Rearing Patterns in Sweden." Golden et al., *New York Infant Day Care Study.* Doyle, "Infant Development in Day Care." Vroegh, "Infant Day Care." M. M. Saunders and M. E. Keister, "Follow-Up Studies of Children Enrolled in a Group Day Care Program in Infancy," unpublished paper, Department of Child Development and Family Relations, University of North Carolina, Greensboro, 1979. Clarke-Stewart and Fein, "Programs for Young Children."

14. Golden et al., *New York City Infant Day Care Study.*
15. Clarke-Stewart, "Predicting Child Development from Child Care Forms and Features." K. A. Clarke-Stewart, C. P. Gruber, and L. M. Fitzgerald, "Predicting Children's Development from Their Experiences at Home and in Day Care," submitted to *Monographs of the Society for Research in Child Development.* K. A. Clarke-Stewart and C. P. Gruber, "Day Care Forms and Features," in R. C. Ainslie, ed., *The Child and the Day Care Setting* (New York: Praeger Special Studies, 1984).
16. H. Goelman and A. R. Pence, "Effects of Child Care, Family, and Individual Characteristics on Children's Language Development: The Victoria Day Care Research Project," in D. A. Phillips, ed., *Quality in Child Care: What Does Research Tell Us?* (Washington, D.C.: NAEYC, 1987).
17. N. Goodman and J. Andrews, "Cognitive Development of Children in Family and Group Day Care," *American Journal of Orthopsychiatry,* 51 (1981), 271–284.
18. E. C. Melhuish, "Research on Day Care for Young Children in the United Kingdom," in E. C. Melhuish and P. Moss, eds., *Day Care for Young Children: International Perspectives* (London and New York: Tavistock/Routledge, 1991). K. McCartney, S. Scarr, D. A. Phillips, S. Grajek, and J. C. Schwarz, "Environmental Differences Among Day Care Centers and their Effects on Children's Development," in E. F. Zigler and E. W. Gordon, eds., *Day Care: Scientific*

and *Social Policy Issues* (Boston: Auburn House, 1982). J. C. Schwarz, G. Krolick, and R. G. Strickland, "Effects of Early Day Care Experience on Adjustment to a New Environment," *American Journal of Orthopsychiatry*, 43 (1973), 340–346. R. Haskins, "Public School Aggression among Children with Varying Day-Care Experience," *Child Development*, 56 (1985), 689–703. T. Field, W. Masi, S. Goldstein, S. Perry, and S. Parl, "Infant Day Care Facilitates Preschool Social Behavior," *Early Childhood Research Quarterly*, 3 (1988), 341–359. Ramey et al., "Preventing Developmental Retardation." Fowler and Khan, *Later Effects of Infant Group Care*. Rubenstein et al., "A Two-Year Follow-Up of Infants in Community Based Day Care." Lally and Honig, "Family Development Research Program." Clarke-Stewart and Fein, "Programs for Young Children."

19. Cochran, "A Comparison of Group Day and Family Child-Rearing Patterns in Sweden." Fowler, *Day Care and Its Effects on Early Development: A Study of Group and Home Care in Multi-Ethnic, Working-Class Families*. Kagan et al., *Infancy: Its Place in Human Development*. Lally and Honig, "The Family Development Research Program." Rubenstein et al., "A Two-Year Follow-Up of Infants in Community Based Day Care." Schwarz et al., "Effects of Early Day Care Experience on Adjustment to a New Environment." M. Siegal and R. M. Storey, "Day Care and Children's Conceptions of Moral and Social Rules," *Child Development*, 56 (1985), 1001–1008. Melhuish, "Research on Day Care for Young Children in the United Kingdom." McCartney et al., "Environmental Differences among Day Care Centers and Their Effects on Children's Development." Schwarz et al., "Effects of Early Day Care Experience on Adjustment to a New Environment." Haskins, "Public School Aggression among Children with Varying Day-Care Experience." Field et al., "Infant Day Care Facilitates Preschool Social Behavior." T. Moore, "Exclusive Early Mothering and Its Alternatives: The Outcomes to Adolescence," *Scandinavian Journal of Psychology*, 16 (1975), 255–272. Clarke-Stewart and Fein, "Programs for Young Children."

20. Steinberg and Green, "Three Types of Day Care."
21. For example, Haskins, "Public School Aggression among Children with Varying Day-Care Experience." Rubenstein and Howes, "Social-Emotional Development of Toddlers in Day Care: The Role of Peers and of Individual Differences." J. C. Schwarz, R. G. Strickland, and G. Krolick, " Infant Day Care: Behavioral Effects at Preschool Age," *Developmental Psychology*, 10 (1974), 502–506. Clarke-Stewart and Fein, "Programs for Young Children." Melhuish, "Research on Day Care for Young Children in the United Kingdom."
22. J. E. Bates, D. Marvinney, D. S. Bennett, K. A. Dodge, T. Kelly, and G. S. Pettit, "Children's Daycare History and Kindergarten Adjustment," paper presented at biennial meeting of the Society for Research in Child Development, Seattle, 1991.
23. K. R. Thornburg, P. Pearl, D. Crompton, and J. M. Ispa, "Development of Kindergarten Children Based on Child Care Arrangements," *Early Childhood Research Quarterly*, 5 (1990), 27–42.
24. Park and Honig, 1991.
25. Belsky et al., "The Ecology of Day Care."
26. Haskins, "Public School Aggression among Children with Varying Day-Care Experience."
27. Bates et al., "Children's Daycare History and Kindergarten Adjustment."
28. N.W. Finkelstein, "Aggression: Is It Stimulated by Day Care?" *Young Children*, 37 (1982), 3–12.
29. Haskins, "Public School Aggression among Children with Varying Day-Care Experience." Field, "Infant Day Care Facilitates Preschool Social Behavior."

6 / PLACES, PROGRAMS, PEERS

1. E. Prescott and T. G. David, "Concept Paper on the Effects of the Physical Environment on Day Care," unpublished paper, Pacific Oaks College, Pasadena, July 1976.
2. W. Rohe and A. H. Patterson, "The Effects of Varied Levels

of Resources and Density on Behavior in a Day Care Center," in D. H. Carson, ed., *Man-Environment Interactions* (New York: Halsted Press, 1975). K. J. Connolly and P. K. Smith, "Experimental Studies of the Preschool Environment," *International Journal of Early Childhood*, 10 (1978), 86–95.

3. Fosburg et al., *National Day Care Home Study*.
4. Clarke-Stewart, "Predicting Child Development from Child Care Forms and Features." C. Howes, "Caregiver Behavior in Centers and Family Day Care," *Journal of Applied Developmental Psychology*, 4 (1983), 99–107. Prescott and David, "Concept Paper on the Effects of the Physical Environment on Day Care."
5. Clarke-Stewart, "Predicting Child Development from Child Care Forms and Features." Connolly and Smith, "Experimental Studies of the Preschool Environment." C. Howes and J. Rubenstein, "Determinants of Toddlers' Experience in Day Care: Age of Entry and Quality of Setting," *Child Care Quarterly*, 14 (1985), 140–151.
6. Prescott and David, "Concept Paper on the Effects of the Physical Environment on Day Care."
7. L. Espinosa, "An Ecological Study of Family Day Care," diss., University of Chicago, 1980. Prescott and David, "Concept Paper on the Effects of the Physical Environment on Day Care."
8. For example, R. Ruopp, J. Travers, F. Glantz, and C. Coelen, *Children at the Center*, final report of the National Day Care Study (Cambridge: Abt Associates, 1979). K. A. Clarke-Stewart, "Interactions between Mothers and Their Young Children: Characteristics and Consequences," *Monographs of the Society for Research in Child Development*, 38 (1973). Golden et al., *New York City Infant Day Care Study*. Clarke-Stewart and Fein, "Programs for Young Children."
9. For example, K. J. Connolly and P. K. Smith, "Experimental Studies of the Preschool Environment," *International Journal of Early Childhood*, 10 (1978), 86–95. J. E. Johnson, J. Ershler, and C. Bell, "Play Behavior in a Discovery-Based

and a Formal-Education Preschool Program," *Child Development,* 51 (1980), 271–274. L. B. Miller and J. L. Dyer, "Four Preschool Programs: Their Dimensions and Effects," *Monographs of the Society for Research in Child Development,* 40 (1975).

10. Sylva et al., *Child Watching at Play Group and Nursery School.*
11. Connolly and Smith, "Experimental Studies of the Preschool Environment."
12. Reviewed by R. S. Soar and R. M. Soar, "An Attempt to Identify Measures of Teacher Effectiveness from Four Studies," paper presented at meeting of the American Educational Research Association, San Francisco, April 1976.
13. Miller and Dyer, "Four Preschool Programs."
14. Haskins, "Public School Aggression among Children with Varying Day-Care Experience."
15. A. Doyle, J. Connolly, and L.-P. Rivest, "The Effects of Playmate Familiarity on the Social Interactions of Young Children," *Child Development,* 51 (1980), 217–223. J. L. Rubenstein and C. Howes, "Caregiving and Infant Behavior in Day Care and in Homes," *Developmental Psychology,* 15 (1979), 1–24. M. Lewis, G. Young, J. Brooks, and L. Michaelson, "The Beginning of Friendship," in M. Lewis and L. A. Rosenblum, eds., *Friendship and Peer Relations* (New York: Wiley-Interscience, 1975).
16. J. M. T. Becker, "A Learning Analysis of the Development of Peer-Oriented Behavior in Nine-Month-Old Infants," *Developmental Psychology,* 13 (1977), 481–491.
17. A. F. Lieberman, "Preschoolers' Competence with a Peer: Relations with Attachment and Peer Experience," *Child Development,* 48 (1977), 1277–87.
18. Sylva et al., *Child Watching at Play Group and Nursery School.*
19. Ruopp et al., *Children at the Center.*
20. Howes, "Caregiver Behavior in Centers and Family Day Care." Howes and Rubenstein, "Determinants of Toddlers' Experience in Day Care." S. D. Holloway and M. Reichhart-Erickson, "The Relationship of Day Care Quality to

Children's Free-Play Behavior and Social Problem-Solving Skills," *Early Childhood Research Quarterly*, 3 (1988), 39–53. Ruopp et al., *Children at the Center.* Sylva et al., *Child Watching at Play Group and Nursery School.* Connolly and Smith, "Experimental Studies of the Preschool Environment." Whitebook et al., *Who Cares?*

21. Connolly and Smith, "Experimental Studies of the Preschool Environment." Ruopp et al., *Children at the Center.* Sylva et al., *Child Watching at Play Group and Nursery School.* Lazar et al., "The Persistence of Preschool Effects." Golden et al., *New York City Infant Day Care Study.*

22. Whitebook et al., *Who Cares?*

23. Clarke-Stewart, "Predicting Child Development from Child Care Forms and Features." K. McCartney, "Effect of Quality of Day Care Environment on Children's Language Development." *Developmental Psychology*, 20 (1984), 244–260. D. A. Phillips, S. Scarr, and K. McCartney, "Dimensions and Effects of Child Care Quality: The Bermuda Study," in D. A. Phillips, ed., *Quality in Child Care: What Does Research Tell Us?* (Washington, D.C.: National Association for the Education of Young Children, 1987).

24. S. B. Greenberg and L. F. Peck, "A Study of Pre-Schoolers' Spontaneous Social Interaction Patterns in Three Settings: All Female, All Male, and Coed," paper presented at meeting of the American Educational Research Association, Chicago, 1974.

25. For example, E. K. Beller, "Infant Day Care: A Longitudinal Study," Office of Child Development (OCD-CB-310), 1974. Fosburg et al., *National Day Care Home Study.* W. W. Hartup, "Children and Their Friends," in H. McGurk, ed., *Issues in Childhood Social Development* (London: Methuen, 1978). Clarke-Stewart and Fein, "Programs for Young Children."

7 / CAREGIVERS

1. J. Carew, "Experience and the Development of Intelligence in Young Children." *Monographs of the Society for Research*

in Child Development, 45 (1980). Clarke-Stewart, "Predicting Child Development from Child Care Forms and Features." Clarke-Stewart "Predicting Children's Development from their Experiences at Home and in Day Care." Clarke-Stewart and Gruber, "Day Care Forms and Features." Golden et al., *New York City Infant Day Care Study.* McCartney, "Effect of Quality of Day Care Environment on Children's Language Development." Phillips et al., "Dimensions and Effects of Child Care Quality." Tyler and Dittmann, "Meeting the Toddler More than Halfway." Lazar et al., "The Persistence of Preschool Effects." Fosburg et al., *National Day Care Home Study.* Espinosa, "An Ecological Study of Family Day Care." D. G. Klinzing and D. R. Klinzing, "An Examination of the Verbal Behavior, Knowledge, and Attitudes of Day Care Teachers," *Education,* 95 (1974), 65–71.

2. Whitebook et al., *Who Cares?*
3. J. Arnett, "Caregivers in Day-Care Centers: Does Training Matter?" *Journal of Applied Developmental Psychology,* 10 (1989), 541–552. Clarke-Stewart, "Predicting Child Development from Child Care Forms and Features." Howes, "Caregiver Behavior in Centers and Family Day Care." Ruopp et al., *Children at the Center.* Whitebook et al., *Who Cares?*
4. Klinzing and Klinzing, "An Examination of the Verbal Behavior, Knowledge, and Attitudes of Day Care Teachers."
5. Whitebook et al., *Who Cares?*
6. Ibid.
7. K. A. Clarke-Stewart, C. P. Gruber, and L. M. Fitzgerald, "Predicting Children's Development from their Experiences at Home and in Day Care," submitted to *Monographs of the Society for Research in Child Development.* Howes, "Caregiver Behavior in Centers and Family Day Care." S. Kontos and R. Fiene, "Child Care Quality, Compliance with Regulations, and Children's Development: The Pennsylvania Study," in D. A. Phillips, ed., *Quality in Child Care: What Does Research Tell Us?* (Washington, D.C.: NAEYC, 1987).

8. Kontos and Fiene, "Child Care Quality, Compliance with Regulations, and Children's Development." Phillips et al., "Dimensions and Effects of Child Care Quality." Ruopp et al., *Children at the Center.*

9. For example, D. Gold, M. Reis, and C. Berger, "Male Teachers and the Development of Nursery School Children," *Psychological Reports,* 44 (1979), 457–458.

10. S. Ambron, "Day Care and Early Social Development," unpublished paper, Boys Town Center for the Study of Youth Development, Stanford University, 1980. Emlen et al., *Child Care by Kith.* Clarke-Stewart, "Predicting Child Development from Child Care Forms and Features." Bryant et al., *Children and Minders.*

11. Clarke-Stewart, "Predicting Child Development from Child Care Forms and Features." Fosburg et al., *National Day Care Home Study.* Steinberg and Green, "Three Types of Day Care."

12. E. M. Cummings, "Caregiver Stability and Day Care," *Developmental Psychology,* 61 (1980), 31–37. J. L. Rubenstein, F. A. Pedersen, and L. J. Yarrow, "What Happens When Mother Is Away: A Comparison of Mothers and Substitute Caregivers," *Developmental Psychology,* 13 (1977), 529–530.

13. T. W. Moore, "Effects on the Children," in S. Yudkin and A. Holme, eds., *Working Mothers and Their Children* (London: Sphere Books, 1969).

14. For example, B. Vaughn, B. Egeland, and L. A. Sroufe, "Individual Differences in Infant-Mother Attachment at Twelve and Eighteen Months: Stability and Change in Families Under Stress," *Child Development,* 50 (1979), 971–975.

15. R. R. Largman, "The Social-Emotional Effects of Age of Entry into Full-Time Group Care," diss., University of California, Berkeley, 1976.

16. Whitebook et al., *Who Cares?*

17. Clarke-Stewart et al., "Predicting Children's Development."

18. For documentation, see the general review by K. A. Clarke-Stewart and N. Apfel, "Evaluating Parental Effects on

Child Development," in L. S. Shulman, ed., *Review of Research in Education*, vol. 6 (Itasca: Peacock, 1979).

19. F. Pedersen, R. Cain, M. Zaslow, and B. Anderson, "Variation in Infant Experience Associated with Alternative Family Role Organization," paper presented at International Conference on Infancy Studies, New Haven, April 1980.

20. M. J. Zaslow, F. A. Pedersen, J. T. D. Suwalsky, R. L. Cain, and M. Fivel, "The Early Resumption of Employment by Mothers: Implications for Parent-Infant Interaction," *Journal of Applied Developmental Psychology*, 6 (1985), 1–16.

21. E. Hock, "Working and Nonworking Mothers and Their Infants: A Comparative Study of Maternal Caregiving Characteristics and Infant Social Behavior," *Merrill-Palmer Quarterly*, 26 (1980), 79–102. S. E. Cohen, "Maternal Employment and Mother-Child Interaction," *Merrill-Palmer Quarterly*, 24 (1978), 189–197. J. B. Schubert, S. Bradley-Johnson, and J. Nuttall, "Mother-Infant Communication and Maternal Employment," *Child Development*, 51 (1980), 246–249.

22. Harrell and Ridley, "Substitute Child Care, Maternal Employment and the Quality of Mother-Child Interaction." Yarrow et al., "Child Rearing in Families of Working and Nonworking Mothers." Hoffman, "Maternal Employment and the Young Child."

23. E. Hock, "Alternative Approaches to Child Rearing and Their Effects on the Mother-Infant Relationship," report (OCD-CB-490) to the Office of Child Development, Department of Health, Education, and Welfare, 1976. E. Hock and J. B. Clinger, "Behavior toward Mother and Stranger of Infants Who Have Experienced Group Day Care, Individual Day Care, or Exclusive Maternal Care," *Journal of Genetic Psychology*, 137 (1980), 49–61.

24. Schubert et al., "Mother-Infant Communication and Maternal Employment."

25. L. W. Hoffman, "Effects of Maternal Employment on the Child—A Review of the Research," *Development Psychol-*

ogy, 10 (1974), 204–1228. Hoffman, "Maternal Employment and the Young Child."

26. A. M. Farel, "Effects of Preferred Maternal Roles, Maternal Employment, and Sociodemographic Status on School Adjustment and Competence," *Child Development,* 51 (1980), 1179–86.

27. R. D. Hess, G. C. Price, W. P. Dickson, and M. Conroy, "Different Roles for Mothers and Teachers: Contrasting Styles of Child Care," in S. Kilmer, ed., *Advances in Early Education and Day Care* (Greenwich: JAI Press 1980).

28. Rubenstein and Howes, "Caregiving and Infant Behavior in Day Care and in Homes." B. Tizard, H. Carmichael, M. Hughes, and G. Pinkerton, "Four Year Olds Talking to Mothers and Teachers," in L. A. Hersov and M. Berger, eds., *Language and Language Disorders in Childhood,* supplement no. 2, *Journal of Child Psychology and Psychiatry* (London: Pergamon Press, 1980). Cochran, "A Comparison of Group Day and Family Child-Rearing Patterns in Sweden." C. S. Winetsky, "Comparison of the Expectations of Parents and Teachers for the Behavior of Preschool Children," *Child Development,* 49 (1978), 1146–54.

29. Tizard et al., "Four Year Olds Talking to Mothers and Teachers."

30. Cochran, "A Comparison of Group and Family Child-Rearing Patterns in Sweden." Clarke-Stewart, "Predicting Child Development from Child Care Forms and Features." Rubenstein et al., "What Happens When Mother Is Away." Bryant et al., *Children and Minders.*

8 / INFANTS AND INDIVIDUALS

1. For example, E. E. Maccoby and C. N. Jacklin, *The Psychology of Sex Differences* (Stanford: Stanford University Press, 1974).

2. Cochran, "A Comparison of Group and Family-Rearing Patterns in Sweden."

3. R. L. Wynn, "The Effect of a Playmate on Day-Care and

Home-Reared Toddlers in a Strange Situation," paper presented at meeting of the Society for Research in Child Development, San Francisco, March 1979. Fowler and Khan, *Later Effects of Infant Group Care.* Moore, "Effects on the Children." L. O. Gunnarsson, "Children in Day Care and Family Care in Sweden: A Follow-Up," diss., University of Michigan, 1978. B. I. Fagot, "Consequences of Moderate Cross-Gender Behavior in Preschool Children," *Child Development,* 48 (1977), 902–907. P. K. Smith and M. Green, "Aggressive Behavior in English Nurseries and Play Groups: Sex Differences and Response of Adults," *Child Development,* 46 (1975), 211–214. L. Bourdeau and T. J. Ryan, "Teacher Interaction with Preschool Children: Attitudes, Contacts, and Their Effects," *Canadian Journal of Behavioural Science,* 10 (1978), 283–295.

4. Belsky et al., "The Ecology of Day Care."

5. S. Desai, P. L. Chase-Lansdale, and R. Michael, "Mother or Market? Effects of Maternal Employment on the Intellectual Ability of Four-Year-Old Children," *Demography,* 26 (1989), 545–561. F. L. Mott, "Developmental Effects of Infant Care: The Mediating Role of Gender and Health," *Journal of Social Issues,* 47 (1991), 139–158.

6. K. McCartney and D. A. Phillips, "Motherhood and Child Care," in B. Birns and D. Hay, eds., *The Different Faces of Motherhood* (New York: Plenum, 1988).

7. C. W. Anderson, R. J. Nagle, W. A. Roberts, and J. W. Smith, "Attachment to Substitute Caregivers as a Function of Center Quality and Caregiver Involvement," *Child Development,* 52 (1981), 53–61. H. N. Ricciuti, "Fear and the Development of Social Attachments in the First Year of Life," in M. Lewis and L. A. Rosenblum, eds., *The Origins of Fear* (New York: Wiley, 1974). Cummings, "Caregiver Stability and Day Care."

8. For example, Cummings, "Caregiver Stability and Day Care." Kagan, Kearsley, and Zelazo, *Infancy.* Bryant et al., *Children and Minders.* Ricciuti, "Fear and the Development of Social Attachments in the First Year of Life." D. C.

Farran and C. T. Ramey, "Infant Day Care and Attachment Behaviors toward Mothers and Teachers," *Child Development,* 48 (1977), 1112–16.

9. K. A. Clarke-Stewart, "Infant Day Care: Maligned or Malignant?" *American Psychologist,* 44 (1989), 266–273.
10. M. van IJzendoorn and P. M. Kroonenberg, "Cross-Cultural Patterns of Attachment: A Meta-Analysis of the Strange Situation," *Child Development,* 59 (1988), 147–156.
11. Melhuish, "Research on Day Care for Young Children in the United Kingdom."
12. Whitebook et al., *Who Cares?*
13. Howes, "Caregiver Behavior in Centers and Family Day Care." Howes and Rubenstein, "Determinants of Toddlers' Experience in Day Care." C. Howes, C. Rodning, D. C. Galluzzo, and L. Myers, "Attachment and Child Care: Relationships with Mother and Caregiver," *Early Childhood Research Quarterly,* 3 (1988), 403–416. Phillips et al., "Dimensions and Effects of Child Care Quality." Ruopp et al., *Children at the Center.*
14. M. C. Blehar, "Mother-Child Interaction in Day-Care and Home-Reared Children," in R. A. Webb, ed., *Social Development in Childhood: Day-Care Programs and Research* (Baltimore: Johns Hopkins University Press, 1977). Bryant et al., *Children and Minders.* Largman, "The Social-Emotional Effects of Age of Entry into Full-Time Group Care."
15. Golden et al., *New York City Infant Day Care Study.* Robinson and Robinson, "Longitudinal Development of Very Young Children in a Comprehensive Day Care Program." Clarke-Stewart, "Predicting Child Development from Child Care Forms and Features." Ruopp et al., *Children at the Center.* E. Ferri, "Combined Nursery Centres," *Concern,* National Children's Bureau, no. 37 (1980).
16. Osborn and Milbank, *Effects of Early Education.*
17. Ramey et al., "Preventing Developmental Retardation."
18. J. Marcus, S. Chess, and A. Thomas, "Temperamental Individuality in Group Care of Young Children," *Early Child Development and Care,* 1 (1972), 313–330.

19. Mott, "Developmental Effects of Infant Care: The Mediating Role of Gender and Health."
20. Robinson and Robinson, "Longitudinal Development of Very Young Children in a Comprehensive Day Care Program." C. Mermilliod, and C. Rossignol, "Le Developpement de l'enfant à 4 ans: Est-il significatif des modes de garde antérieur?" *Bulletin de statistiques,* 2 (1974), 105–131.
21. Garber and Heber, "Modification of Predicted Cognitive Development in High-Risk Children through Early Intervention." Cochran, "A Comparison of Group and Family Child-Rearing Patterns in Sweden."
22. Bryant et al., *Children and Minders.* Howes and Rubenstein, "Prediction of Infant Adaptation to Day Care." R. P. Klein and J. T. Durfee, "Prediction of Preschool Social Behavior from Social-Emotional Development at One Year," *Child Psychiatry and Human Development,* 9 (1979), 145–151. M. A. Easterbrooks and M. E. Lamb, "The Relationship between Quality of Infant-Mother Attachment and Infant Competence in Initial Encounters with Peers," *Child Development,* 50 (1979), 380–387.

9 / FINDING GOOD CARE

1. J. Frost and H. Schneider, *Types of Day Care and Parents' Preferences,* final report, part 7 (ERIC, 1971, ED 068 195). C.R. Hill, *The Child Care Market: A Review of the Evidence and Implications for Federal Policy* (ERIC 1977, ED 156 352). Dickinson, *Child Care.* Emlen et al., *Child Care by Kith.*
2. Steinberg and Green, "Three Types of Day Care." S. Low and P. G. Spindler, "Child Care Arrangements of Working Mothers in the United States," U.S. Children's Bureau and U.S. Women's Bureau, 1968. F. A. Ruderman, *Child Care and Working Mothers: A Study of Arrangements Made for Daytime Care of Children* (New York: Child Welfare League of America, 1963).
3. Emlen et al., *Child Care by Kith.*
4. Ruopp et al., *Children at the Center.* Ruderman, *Child Care and Working Mothers.*

5. D. R. Powell, with J. W. Eisenstadt, "Finding Child Care: A Study of Parents' Search Processes," report for the Ford Foundation (780–0372), June 1980.

6. Powell and Eisenstadt, "Finding Child Care." M. R. Bradbard and R. C. Endsley, "What Do Licensers Say to Parents Who Ask Their Help with Selecting Quality Day Care?" *Child Care Quarterly,* 8 (1979), 307–312. S. Auerbach-Fink, "Mothers' Expectations of Child Care," *Young Children,* 32 (1977), 12–21.

7. Bone, *Preschool Children and the Need for Day Care.* Ruderman, *Child Care and Working Mothers.* Frost and Schneider, *Types of Day Care and Parents' Preferences.* Steinberg and Green, "Three Types of Day Care." E. Handler and J. Fredlund, *Differences between Highly Satisfied and Not Highly Satisfied Clients of Day Care Centers* (ERIC, 1971, ED 068 165).

8. Whitebook et al., *Who Cares?*

9. Bradbard and Endsley, "What Do Licensers Say to Parents Who Ask Their Help with Selecting Quality Day Care?"

10. R. H. Passman, "Mothers and Blankets as Agents for Promoting Play and Exploration by Young Children in a Novel Environment: The Effects of Social and Nonsocial Attachment Objects," *Developmental Psychology,* 11 (1975), 170–177. N. G. Blurton-Jones and G. Leach, "Behaviour of Children and Their Mothers at Separation and Greeting," in N. G. Blurton-Jones, ed., *Ethological Studies of Child Behavior* (Cambridge: Cambridge University Press, 1972). M. Kotelchuck, P. R. Zelazo, J. Kagan, and E. Spelke, "Infant Reactions to Parental Separations When Left with Familiar and Unfamiliar Adults," *Journal of Genetic Psychology,* 126 (1975), 255–262. C. M. Heinicke and I. Westheimer, *Brief Separations* (New York: International Press, 1965). M. Weinraub and M. Lewis, "The Determinants of Children's Responses to Separation," *Monographs of the Society for Research in Child Development,* 42 (1977). J. C. Schwarz and R. Wynn. "The Effects of Mother's Presence and Previsits on Children's Emotional Reaction to Starting Nursery School," *Child Development,* 42 (1971), 871–881.

10 / ALTERNATIVES

1. More about daycare in these and other countries can be found in U. Bronfenbrenner, *Two Worlds of Childhood: U.S. and U.S.S.R.* (New York: Basic Books, 1970). W. Kessen, *Childhood in China* (New Haven: Yale University Press, 1975). Robinson et al., *A World of Children.* P. P. Olmsted and D. P. Weikart, *How Nations Serve Young Children: Profiles of Child Care and Education in 14 Countries* (Ypsilanti: High/Scope, 1989). E. C. Melhuish and P. Moss, *Day Care for Young Children: International Perspectives* (New York: Routledge, 1991). S. B. Kamerman, "Child Care Policies and Programs: An International Overview," *Journal of Social Issues,* 47 (1991), 179–196.
2. N. B. Kupriyanova and T. N. Fedosdeeva, "Play and Activity for Children in the First Three Years of Life," cited in J. Marcus, ed., *Growing Up in Groups: The Russian Day Care Center and the Israeli Kibbutz: Two Manuals on Early Childcare* (New York: Gordon and Breach, 1972).
3. Y. Ben-Yaakov, "Methods of Kibbutz Collective Education during Early Childhood," cited in Marcus, *Growing Up in Groups.*
4. For example, B. Beit-Hallahmi and A. I. Rabin, "The Kibbutz as a Social Experiment and as a Child-Rearing Laboratory," *American Psychologist,* 32 (1977), 532–541. A. Avgar, U. Bronfenbrenner, and C. R. Henderson, "Socialization Practices of Parents, Teachers, and Peers in Israel: Kibbutz, Moshav, and City," *Child Development,* 48 (1977), 1219–27. H. T. Nahir and R. S. Yussen, "The Performance of Kibbutz- and City-Reared Israeli Children on Two Role-Taking Tasks," *Developmental Psychology,* 13 (1977), 450–455. E. Regev, B. Beit-Hallahmi, and R. Sharabay, "Affective Expression in Kibbutz-Communal, Kibbutz-Familial, and City-Raised Children in Israel," *Child Development,* 51 (1980), 232–237.

11 / THE FUTURE

1. Lou Harris and Associates, "Families at Work: Strengths and Strains," *General Mills American Family Forum* (Minneapolis: General Mills, 1981).
2. S. B. Kamerman, A. J. Kahn, and P. W. Kingston, *Maternity Policies and Working Women* (New York: Columbia University Press, 1983).
3. Galinsky, "Family Life and Corporate Policies."
4. Whitebook et al., *Who Cares?*
5. Goelman and Pence, "Effects of Child Care, Family, and Individual Characteristics on Children's Language Development." Fosburg et al., *National Day Care Home Study.* Kisker et al., *Profile of Child Care Settings.*

Suggested Reading

Edward C. Melhuish and Peter Moss, eds., *Day Care for Young Children: International Perspectives* (London: Tavistock; New York: Routledge, 1991). A collection of essays describing daycare services in France, Germany, Sweden, England, and the United States and reviewing the research done on the effects of daycare in each of these countries.

Peter Moss and Edward Melhuish, eds., *Current Issues in Day Care for Young Children* (London: HMSO, 1991). The papers in this book were originally prepared for a conference sponsored by the Department of Health in the United Kingdom, addressed to daycare providers. They discuss issues of daycare research and policy in England, Sweden, and the United States.

Jo Ann Miller and Susan Weissman, *The Parents' Guide to Daycare* (New York: Bantam, 1986). This is a practical guide for parents. Its ambitious subtitle promises, "Everything you need to know to find the best care for your child and to make it happy, safe and problem-free from day to day."

Shahla S. Chehrazi, ed., *Psychosocial Issues in Day Care* (Washington, D.C.: American Psychiatric Press, 1990). A collection by experts in the field of daycare, offering detailed reviews of research and insightful suggestions by clinicians.

Faye J. Crosby, *Juggling: The Unexpected Advantages of Balancing Career and Home for Women and Their Families* (New York:

Free Press; Oxford: Maxwell MacMillan International, 1991). An articulate and sympathetic presentation of the case for working mothers. It draws on research on women, families, and work and on personal anecdotes and interviews.

Cheryl D. Hayes, John L. Palmer, and Martha J. Zaslow, eds., *Who Cares for America's Children? Childcare Policy for the 1990s* (Washington, D.C.: National Academy Press, 1990). An authoritative volume written by a blue-ribbon panel of scientists, discussing daycare from the perspectives of economics, policy, service, and research.

Sandra Scarr and Judy Dunn, *Mother Care/Other Care: The Child-Care Dilemma for Women and Children* (New York: Basic Books, 1984; Harmondsworth: Penguin, 1987). A well-written overview that places daycare in the context of what is best for children and mothers.

Nathan Fox and Greta G. Fein, eds., *Infant Day Care: The Current Debate.* (Norwood: Ablex, 1990). For the academically inclined, a collection of research articles debating the evidence on effects of daycare on children's social and emotional development.

Deborah A. Phillips, ed., *Quality in Childcare: What Does Research Tell Us?* (Washington, D.C.: National Association for the Education of Young Children, 1987). A summary of several studies written originally for daycare practitioners.

Fredelle Maynard, *The Child Care Crisis* (Markham, Ontario: Penguin Books/Viking, 1985). A detailed discussion directed to parents.

Richard Endsley and Marilyn Bradbard, *Quality Day Care. A Handbook of Choices for Parents and Caregivers* (Englewood Cliffs: Prentice-Hall, 1981). A useful guide for parents choosing among available daycare facilities.

Index